BOOKS AND PLAY-BOOKS.

BOOKS AND PLAY-BOOKS

ESSAYS ON LITERATURE AND

THE DRAMA

BY

BRANDER MATTHEWS

Essay Index Reprint Series

BOOKS FOR LIBRARIES PRESS
FREEPORT, NEW YORK

First Published 1895
Reprinted 1972

Library of Congress Cataloging in Publication Data

Matthews, Brander, 1852-1929.
  Books and play-books.

  (Essay index reprint series)
  Reprint of the 1895 ed.
  CONTENTS: The evolution of copyright.--The dramatization of novels.--On certain parallelisms between
the ancient and the modern drama. ⌈etc.⌉
  1. Literature--Addresses, essays, lectures.
2. Literature, Modern--19th century--Addresses, essays,
lectures. 3. Drama--Addresses, essays, lectures.
I. Title.
PN761.M3 1972   809   71-37795
ISBN 0-8369-2612-9

PRINTED IN THE UNITED STATES OF AMERICA
BY
NEW WORLD BOOK MANUFACTURING CO., INC.
HALLANDALE, FLORIDA 33009

CONTENTS.

BOOKS & PLAY-BOOKS.

THE EVOLUTION OF COPYRIGHT.

" THE only thing that divides us on the question of copyright seems to be a question as to how much property there is in books," said Lowell, two or three years ago ; and he continued,

" but that is a question we may be well content to waive till we have decided that there is any property at all in them. I think that, in order that the two sides should come together, nothing more is necessary than that both should understand clearly that property, whether in books or in land or in anything else, is artificial ; that it is purely a creature of law ; and, more than that, of local and municipal law. When we have come to an agreement of this sort, I think we shall not find it difficult to come to an agreement that it will be best for us to get whatever acknowledgment of property we can, in books, to start with."

" An author has no natural right to a property in his production," said the late

Matthew Arnold, in his acute and suggestive essay on copyright,

" but then neither has he a natural right to anything whatever which he may produce or acquire. What is true is that a man has a strong instinct making him seek to possess what he has produced or acquired, to have it at his own disposal; that he finds pleasure in so having it, and finds profit. The instinct is natural and salutary, although it may be over-stimulated and indulged to excess. One of the first objects of men, in combining themselves in society, has been to afford to the individual, in his pursuit of this instinct, the sanction and assistance of the laws, so far as may be consistent with the general advantage of the community. The author, like other people, seeks the pleasure and the profit of having at his own disposal what he produces. Literary production, wherever it is sound, is its own exceeding great reward; but that does not destroy or diminish the author's desire and claim to be allowed to have at his disposal, like other people, that which he produces, and to be free to turn it to account. It happens that the thing which he produces is a thing hard for him to keep at his own disposal, easy for other people to appropriate; but then, on the other hand, he is an interesting producer, giving often a great deal of pleasure by what he produces, and not provoking Nemesis by any huge and immoderate profits on his production, even when it is suffered to be at his own disposal. So society has taken him under its protection, and has sanctioned his property in his work, and enabled him to have it at his own disposal."

Perhaps a consideration of the evolution of copyright in the past will conduce to a closer understanding of its condition at present, and to a clearer appreciation of its probable development in the future. It is instructive as well as entertaining to trace the steps by which men, combining themselves in society, in Arnold's phrase, have afforded to the individual author the sanction of the law in possessing what he has produced ; and it is no less instructive to note the successive enlargements of jurisprudence by which property in books—which is, as Lowell says, the creature of local municipal law—has slowly developed until it demands and receives international recognition.

I.

The maxim that "there is no wrong without a remedy," indicates the line of legal development. The instinct of possession is strong ; and in the early communities, where most things were in common, it tended more and more to assert itself. When anything which a man claimed as his own was taken from him, he had a sense of wrong, and his first movement was to seek vengeance—much as a dog defends his bone, growling when it is taken from him, or even biting. If public opinion supported the claim of possession, the claimant would be sustained in his effort to get revenge. So, from the admission of a wrong, would grow up the recognition of a right. The moral right became a legal right as soon as it received the sanction of the State. The State first commuted the right of vengeance, and awarded damages, and the action of tort was born. For a long period property was protected only by the action for damages for disseizin ; but this action steadily widened in scope until it became an action for recovery ; and the idea of possession or seizin broadened into the idea of ownership. This development went on slowly, bit by bit and day by day, under the influence of individual self-assertion and the resulting pressure of public opinion, which, as Lowell once tersely put it, is like that of the atmosphere : " You can't see it, but it is fifteen pounds to the square inch all the same."

The individual sense of wrong stimulates the moral growth of society at large ; and in due course of time, after a strenuous struggle with those who profit by the denial of justice, there comes a calm at last, and ethics crystal-lize into law. In more modern periods of development, the recognition of new forms of property generally passes through three stages. First, there is a mere moral right, asserted by the individual and admitted by most other individuals, but not acknowledged by society as a whole. Second, there is a desire on the part of those in authority to find some means of protection for this admitted moral right, and the action in equity is allowed—this being an effort to command the conscience of those whom the ordinary policeman is incompetent to deal with. And thirdly, in the fulness of time, there is declared a law setting forth clearly the privileges of the producer and the means whereby he can defend his property and recover damages for an attack on it. This process of legislative declaration of rights is still going on all about us and in all departments of law, as modern life develops and spreads out and becomes more and more complex ; and we have come to a point where we can accept Jhering's definition of a legal right as " a legally protected interest."

As it happens, this growth of a self-asserted claim into a legally protected interest can be traced with unusual ease in the evolution of copyright, because copyright itself is comparatively a new thing. The idea of property was probably first recognized in the tools which early man made for himself, and in the animals or men whom he subdued ; later, in the soil which he cultivated. In the beginning the idea attached only to tangible things—to actual physical possession—to that which a man might pass from hand to hand. Now, in the dawn of history nothing was less a physical possession than literature ; it was not only intangible, it was invisible even. There was literature before there was any writing, before an author could set down his lines in black and white. Homer and the rhapsodists published their poems by word of mouth. *Litera scripta manet ;* but the spoken poem flew away with the voice of the speaker and lingered only in the memory. Even after writing was invented, and after parchment and papyrus made it possible to preserve the labours of the poet and the historian, these authors had not, for many a century yet, any thought of making money by multiplying copies of their works.

The Greek dramatists, like the dramatists of to-day, relied for their pecuniary reward on the public performance of their plays. There is a tradition that Herodotus, when an old man, read his "History" to an Athenian audience at the Panathenaic festival, and so delighted them that they gave him as a recompense ten talents—more than twelve thousand dollars of our money. In Rome, where there were booksellers having scores of trained slaves to transcribe manuscripts for sale, perhaps the successful author was paid for a poem, but we find no trace of copyright or of anything like it. Horace ("Ars Poetica," 345) speaks of a certain book as likely to make money for a certain firm of booksellers. In the other Latin poets, and even in the prose writers of

Rome, we read more than one cry of suffering over the blunders of the copyists, and more than one protest in anger against the mangled manuscripts of the hurried, servile transcribers. But nowhere do we find any complaint that the author's rights have been infringed ; and this, no doubt, was because the author did not yet know that he had any wrongs. Indeed, it was only after the invention of printing that an author had an awakened sense of the injury done him in depriving him of the profit of vending his own writings ; because it was only after Gutenberg had set up as a printer that the possibility of definite profit from the sale of his works became visible to the author. Before then he had felt no sense of wrong ; he had thought mainly of the honour of a wide circulation of his writings ; and he had been solicitous chiefly about the exactness of the copies. With the invention of printing there was a chance of profit ; and as soon as the author saw this profit diminished by an unauthorized reprint, he was conscious of injury, and he protested with all the strength that in him lay. He has continued to protest from that day to this ; and public opinion has been aroused, until by slow steps the author is gaining the protection he claims.

It is after the invention of printing that we must seek the origin of copyright. Mr. De Vinne shows that Gutenberg printed a book

with movable types, at Mentz, in 1451. Fourteen years later, in 1465, two Germans began
to print in a monastery near Rome, and removed to Rome itself in 1467 ; and in 1469
John of Spira began printing in Venice.
Louis XI. sent to Mentz Nicholas Jenson,
who introduced the art into France in 1469.
Caxton set up the first press in England in
1474.

In the beginning these printers were publishers also ; most of their first books were
Bibles, prayer-books, and the like ; but in
1465, probably not more than fifteen years
after the first use of movable types, Fust and
Schoeffer put forth an edition of Cicero's
" Offices "—" the first tribute of the new art
to polite literature," Hallam calls it. The
original editing of the works of a classic
author, the comparison of manuscripts, the
supplying of *lacunæ*, the revision of the text,
called for scholarship of a high order ; this
scholarship was sometimes possessed by the
printer-publisher himself ; but more often
than not he engaged learned men to prepare
the work for him and to see it through the
press. This first edition was a true pioneer's
task ; it was a blazing of the path and a clear-
ing of the field. Once done, the labour of
printing again that author's writings in a condition acceptable to students would be easy.
Therefore the printer-publisher who had given

time and money and hard work to the proper
presentation of a Greek or Latin book was
outraged when a rival press sent forth a copy
of his edition, and sold the volume at a lower
price, possibly, because there had been no
need to pay for the scholarship which the first
edition had demanded.   That the earliest
person to feel the need of copyright production should have been a printer-publisher is
worthy of remark ; obviously, in this case, the
printer-publisher stood for the author and was
exactly in his position.   He was prompt to
protest against this disseizin [1] of the fruit of
his labours ; and the earliest legal recognition
of his rights was granted less than a score of
years after the invention of printing had
made the injury possible.   It is pleasant for
us Americans to know that this first feeble
acknowledgment of copyright was made by a
republic.   The Senate of Venice issued an
order, in 1469, that John of Spira should have
the exclusive right for five years to print the
epistles of Cicero and of Pliny. [2]

This privilege was plainly an exceptional

[1] If any lawyer objects to the use of the word "disseizin" in connection with other than real property, he
is referred to Professor J. B. Ames's articles on Disseizin of Chattels, in the "Harvard Law Review,"
January—March, 1890.

[2] Sanuto, "Script. Rerum Itálic.," t. xxii., p. 1189 :
cited by Hallam, "History of Middle Ages," chap. ix.,
part ii.

exercise of the power of the sovereign state to protect the exceptional merit of a worthy citizen ; it gave but a limited protection ; it guarded but two books, for a brief period only, and only within the narrow limits of one commonwealth. But, at least, it established a precedent—a precedent which has broadened down the centuries until now, four hundred years later, any book published in Venice is, by international conventions, protected from pillage for a period of at least fifty years, through a territory which includes almost every important country of continental Europe. If John of Spira were to issue to-day his edition of Tully's " Letters," he need not fear an unauthorized reprint anywhere in the kingdom of which Venice now forms a part, or in his native land, Germany, or in France, Belgium, or Spain, or even in Tunis, Liberia, or Hayti.

The habit of asking for a special privilege from the authorities of the State wherein the book was printed spread rapidly. In 1491 Venice gave the publicist, Peter of Ravenna, and to the publisher of his choice the exclusive right to print and sell his " Phœnix " [1]—the first recorded instance of a copyright awarded directly to an author. Other Italian states " encouraged printing by granting to different

---

[1] Bowker, "Copyright," p. 5.

printers exclusive rights for fourteen years,
more or less, of printing specified classics,"
and thus the time of the protection accorded
to John of Spira was doubled.   In Germany
the first privilege was issued at Nuremberg,
in 1501.   In France the privilege covered but
one edition of a book ; and if the work went
to press again, the publisher had to seek a
second patent.

In England, in 1518, Richard Pynson, the
King's Printer, issued the first book *cum
privilegio ;* the title-page declaring that no
one else should print or import in England
any other copies for two years ; and in 1530 a
privilege for seven years was granted to John
Palsgrave " in the consideration of the value
of his work and the time spent on it ; this
being the first recognition of the nature of
copyright as furnishing a reward to the author
for his labour." [1]   In 1533 Wynkyn de Worde
obtained the king's privilege for his second
edition of Witinton's " Grammar."   The first
edition of this book had been issued ten years
before, and during the decade it had been
reprinted by Peter Trevers without leave—a
despoilment against which Wynkyn de Worde
protested vigorously in the preface to the later
edition, and on account of which he applied
for and secured protection.   Here again is

----

[1] Scrutton, " Laws of Copyright," p. 72.

evidence that a man does not think of his
rights until he feels a wrong. Jhering bases
the struggle for law on the instinct of ownership as something personal, and the feeling
that the person is attacked whenever a man is
deprived of his property; and, as Walter
Savage Landor wrote: "No property is so
entirely and purely and religiously a man's
own as what comes to him immediately from
God, without intervention or participation."
The development of copyright, and especially
its rapid growth within the past century, is
due to the loud protests of authors deprived
of the results of their labours, and therefore
smarting as acutely as under a personal insult.[1]

The invention of printing was almost simul-
taneous with the Reformation, with the discovery of America, and with the first voyage
around the Cape of Good Hope. There was
in those days a ferment throughout Europe,
and men's minds were making ready for a
great outbreak. Of this movement, intellectual on one side and religious on the other,
the governments of the time were afraid; they
saw that the press was spreading broadcast
new ideas which might take root in the most
inconvenient places, and spring up at the most
inopportune moments; so they sought at once
to control the printing of books. In less than

[1] Jhering, "The Struggle for Law" (translated by
J. J. Lalor).

a century after Gutenberg had cast the first
type, the privileges granted for the encourage-
ment and reward of the printer-publisher and
of the author were utilized to enable those in
authority to prevent the sending forth of such
works as they might choose to consider trea-
sonable or heretical.   For a while, therefore,
the history of the development of copyright is
inextricably mixed with the story of press-
censorship.   In France, for example, the edict
of Moulins, in 1566, forbade " any person whatsoever printing or causing to be printed any
book or treatise without leave and permission
of the king, and letters of privilege." [1]   Of
course, no privilege was granted to publisher
or to author if the royal censors did not
approve of the book.

In England the " declared purpose of the
Stationers' Company, chartered by Philip and
Mary in 1556, was to prevent the propagation
of the Protestant Reformation." [2]   The famous
" Decree of Star Chamber concerning print-
ing," issued in 1637, set forth,

" that no person or persons whatsoever shall at any
time print or cause to be imprinted any book or
pamphlet whatsoever, unless the same book or
pamphlet, and also all and every the titles, epistles,
prefaces, proems, preambles, introductions, tables,

[1] Alcide Darras, " Du Droit des Auteurs," p. 169.
[2] Drone, " A Treatise on the Law of Property in
Intellectual Productions," p. 56.

dedications, and other matters and things whatsoever thereunto annexed, or therewith imprinted,
shall be first lawfully licensed."

In his learned introduction to the beautiful
edition of this decree, made by him for the
Grolier Club, Mr. De Vinne remarks that at
this time the people of England were boiling
with discontent; and, "annoyed by a little
hissing of steam," the ministers of Charles I.
" closed all the valves and outlets, but did not
draw or deaden the fires which made the
steam ; " then " they sat down in peace, grati-
fied with their work, just before the explosion
which destroyed them." This decree was
made the eleventh day of July, 1637 ; and in
1641 the Star Chamber was abolished ; and
eight years later the king was beheaded at
Whitehall.

The slow growth of a protection, which was
in the beginning only a privilege granted at
the caprice of the officials, into a legal right,
to be obtained by the author by observing the
simple formalities of registration and deposit,
is shown in a table given in the appendix
(page 370) to the " Report of the Copyright
Commission " (London, 1878). The salient
dates in this table are these:

" 1637.—Star Chamber Decree supporting copy-
    right.
1643.—Ordinance of the Commonwealth concern-

ing licensing.   Copyright maintained, but sub-
ordinate to political objects.

1662.—13 and 14 Car. II., c. 33.—Licensing Act
continued by successive Parliaments; gives
copyright coupled with license.

1710.—8 Anne, c. 19.—First Copyright Act. Copyright to be for fourteen years, and if author
then alive, for fourteen years more.   Power to
regulate price.

1814.—54 Geo. III., c. 156.—Copyright to be for
twenty-eight years absolutely, and further for
the life of the author, if then living.

1842.—5 and 6 Vict., c. 45.—Copyright to be for
the life of the author and seven years longer,
or for forty-two years, whichever term last
expires."

From Mr. Bowker's chapter on the " History
of Copyright in the United States," it is easy
to draw up a similar table showing the development in America :

" 1793.—Connecticut, in January, and Massachusetts, in March, passed acts granting copyrights
for twenty-one years.   In May Congress recommended the States to pass acts granting copyright for fourteen years (seemingly a step
backward from the Connecticut and Massachusetts statutes).

1785 and 1786.—Copyright Acts passed in Virginia,
New York, and New Jersey.

1786.—Adoption of the Constitution of the United
States, authorizing Congress ' to promote the
progress of science and useful arts by securing
for limited times, to authors and inventors, the

exclusive right to their respective writings and discoveries.'

1790.—First United States Copyright Act. Copyright to citizens or residents for fourteen years, with a renewal for fourteen years more if the author were living at the expiration of the first term.

1831.—Copyright to be for twenty-eight years, with a renewal for fourteen years more, if the author, his widow, or his children are living at the expiration of the first term.

1856.—Act securing to dramatists stage-right; that is, the sole right to license the performance of a play.

1873-4.—The Copyright Laws were included in the Revised Statutes (sections 4948 to 4971)."

From the exhaustive and excellent work of M. Lyon-Caen and M. Paul Delalain on "Literary and Artistic Property"[1] we see that France, now, perhaps, the foremost of all nations in the protection it accords to literary property, lagged behind Great Britain and the United States in taking the second step in the evolution of copyright. It was in 1710 that the act of Anne gave the British author a legal right independent of the caprice of any official; and as soon as the United States came into being, the same right was promptly confirmed to our citizens; but it was not until the fall of the ancient *régime* that a French-

---

[1] "La Propriété Littéraire et Artistique : Lois Françaises et Étrangères" (Paris, Pichon, 1889, 2 vols.).

man was enabled to take out a copyright at
will. Up to the eve of the Revolution of 1789,
French authors could do no more, say MM.
Lyon-Caen and Delalain, "than ask for a
privilege which might always be refused them "
(page 8). As was becoming in a country
where the drama has ever been the most important department of literature, the first step
taken was a recognition of the stage-right of
the dramatist, in a law passed in 1791. Before that, a printed play could have been
acted in France by any one, but thereafter the
exclusive right of performance was reserved
to the playwright ; and at one bound the
French went far beyond the limit of time for
which any copyright was then granted either
in England or America, as the duration of
stage-right was to be for the author's life and
for five years more. It is to be noted, also,
that stage-right was not acquired by British
and American authors for many years after
1791.

Two years after the French law protecting
stage-right, in the dark and bloody year of
1793, an act was passed in France granting
copyright for the life of the author and for
ten years after his death. It is worthy of
remark that, as soon as the privileges and
monopolies of the monarchy were abolished,
the strong respect the French people have
always felt for literature and art was shown

C

by the extension of the term of copyright far
beyond that then accorded in Great Britain
and the United States; and although both
the British and the American term of copyright has been prolonged since 1793, so also
has the French, and it is now for life of the
author and for fifty years after his death.

The rapid development of law within the
past century and the effort it makes to keep
pace with the moral sense of society—a sense
that becomes finer as society becomes more
complicated and as the perception of personal
wrong is sharpened—can be seen in this brief
summary of copyright development in France,
where, but a hundred years ago, an author
had only the power of asking for a privilege
which might be refused him. The other
countries of Europe, following the lead of
France as they have been wont to do, have
formulated copyright laws not unlike hers.
In prolonging the duration of the term of
copyright, one country has been even more
liberal. Spain extends it for eighty years
after the author's death. Hungary, Belgium,
and Russia accept the French term of the
author's life and half a century more. Germany, Austria, and Switzerland grant only
thirty years after the author dies. Italy gives
the author copyright for his life, with exclusive control to his heirs for forty years after
his death; after that period the exclusive

rights cease, but a royalty of five per cent. on the retail price of every copy of every edition, by whomsoever issued, must be paid to the author's heirs for a further term of forty years : thus a quasi-copyright is granted for a period extending to eighty years after the author's death, and the Italian term is approximated to the Spanish. Certain of the Spanish-American nations have exceeded the liberality of the mother-country : in Mexico, in Guatemala, and in Venezuela the author's rights are not terminated by the lapse of time, and copyright is perpetual.[1]

To set down with precision what has been done in various countries will help us to see more clearly what remains to be done in our own. It is only by considering the trend of legal development that we can make sure of the direction in which efforts toward improvement can be guided most effectively. For example : the facts contained in the preceding paragraphs show that no one of the great nations of continental Europe grants copyright for a less term than the life of the author and a subsequent period varying from thirty to

[1] Here again it may be noted that certain decisions in the United States courts, to the effect that the performance of a play is not publication, and that therefore an unpublished play is protected by the common law and not by the copyright acts, recognize the perpetual stage-right of any dramatist who will forego the doubtful profit of appearing in print.

eighty years. A comparison also of the laws of the various countries, as contained in the invaluable volumes of MM. Lyon-Caen and Delalain, reveals to us the fact that there is a steady tendency to lengthen this term of years, and that the more recent the legislation the more likely is the term to be long. In Austria, for instance, where the term was fixed in 1846, it is for thirty years after the author's death; while in the twin-kingdom of Hungary, where the term was fixed in 1884, it is for fifty years.

On a contrast of the terms of copyright granted by the chief nations of continental Europe with those granted by Great Britain and the United States, it will be seen that the English-speaking race, which was first to make the change from privilege to copyright, and was thus the foremost in the protection of the author, now lags sadly behind. The British law declares that the term of copyright shall be for the life of the author and only seven years thereafter, or for forty-two years, which-ever term last expires. The American law does not even give an author copyright for the whole of his life, if he should be so unlucky as to survive forty-two years after the publica-tion of his earlier books; it grants copyright for twenty-eight years only, with a permission to the author himself, his widow, or his children to renew for fourteen years more. This is

niggardly when set beside the liberality of
France, to say nothing of that of Italy and
Spain. Those who are unwilling to concede
that the ethical development of France, Italy,
and Spain is more advanced than that of
Great Britain and the United States, at least
as far as literary property is concerned, may
find some comfort in recalling the fact that
the British act was passed in 1842 and the
American in 1831—and in threescore years
the world moves.

There is no need to dwell on the disadvantages of the existing American law, and on
the injustice which it works. It may take
from an author the control of his book at the
very moment when he is at the height of his
fame and when the infirmities of age make
the revenue from his copyrights most necessary. An example or two from contemporary
American literature will serve to show the de-
merits of the existing law. The first part of
Bancroft's " History of the United States,"
the history of the colonization, was published
in three successive volumes in 1834, 1837, and
1840 ; and although the author, before his
death, revised and amended this part of his
work, it has been lawful, since 1882, for any
man to take the unrevised and incorrect first
edition and to reprint it, despite the protests
of the author, and in competition with the improved version which contains the results of

the author's increased knowledge and keener taste.

At this time of writing (1890) all books published in the United States prior to 1848 are open to any reprinter ; and the reprinter has not been slow to avail himself of this permission. The children of Fenimore Cooper are alive, and so are the nieces of Washington Irving ; but they derive no income from the rival reprints of the " Leatherstocking Tales " or of the " Sketch Book," reproduced from the earliest editions without any of the authors' later emendations.[1] Though the family of Cooper and the family of Irving survive, Cooper and Irving are dead themselves, and cannot protest. But there are living American authors besides Bancroft who are despoiled in like manner. Half-a-dozen volumes were published by Mr. Whittier and by Dr. Holmes before 1848, and these early, immature, uncorrected verses are now reprinted and offered to the public as "Whittier's Poems" and "Holmes's Poems." Sometimes the tree of poesy flowers early and bears fruit late. So it is with Lowell, whose " Heartease and Rue " we received with delight only a year or two ago, but whose " Legend of Brittany," " Vision of Sir Launfal," " Fable for Critics " and first series of " Biglow Papers " were all published

[1] The emendations, having been made within forty-two years, are, of course, still guarded by copyright.

forty-two years ago or more, and are therefore no longer the property of their author, but have passed from his control absolutely and forever.

Besides the broadening of a capricious privilege into a legal right, and besides the lengthening of the time during which this right is enforced, a steady progress of the idea that the literary labourer is worthy of his hire is to be seen in various newer and subsidiary developments. With the evolution of copyright, the author can now reserve certain secondary rights of abridgment, of adaptation, and of translation. In all the leading countries of the world the dramatist can now secure stage-right,[1] *i.e.*, the sole right to authorize the performance of a play on a stage. Copyright and stage-right are wholly different; and a dramatist is entitled to both. The author of a play has made something which may be capable of a double use, and it seems proper that he should derive profit from both uses. His play may be read only and not acted, like Lord Tennyson's " Harold " and Longfellow's " Spanish Student," in which case the copyright is more valuable than the stage-right. Or the play may be acted only, like the im-

[1] Mr. Drone uses the word "playright," but this is identical in sound with "playwright," and it seems better to adopt the word "stage-right," first employed by Charles Reade.

ported British melodramas, and of so slight a
literary merit that no one would care to read
it, in which case the stage-right would be
more valuable than the copyright.   Or the
drama may be both readable and actable, like
Shakespeare's and Sheridan's plays, like
Augier's and Labiche's, in which case the
author derives a double profit, controlling the
publication by copyright and controlling performance by stage-right.   It was in 1791, as
we have seen, that France granted stage-right.
In England, "the first statute giving to dramatists the exclusive right of performing their
plays was the 3 and 4 William IV., c. 15,
passed in 1833," says Mr. Drone (page 601).
In the United States, stage-right was granted
in 1851 to dramatists who had copyrighted
their plays here.

Closely akin to the stage-right accorded to
the dramatist is the sole right of dramatization accorded to the novelist.   Indeed, the
latter is an obvious outgrowth of the former.
Until the enormous increase of the reading
public in this century, consequent upon the
spread of education, the novel was an inferior
form to the drama and far less profitable
pecuniarily.   It is only within the past
hundred years—one might say, fairly enough,
that it is only since the Waverley novels took
the world by storm—that the romance has
claimed equality with the play.   Until it did

so, no novelist felt wronged when his tale
was turned to account on the stage, and no
novelist ever thought of claiming a sole right
to the theatrical use of his own story. Lodge,
the author of " Rosalynde," would have been
greatly surprised if any one had told him that
Shakespeare had made an improper use of
his story in founding on it " As You Like It."
On the contrary, in fact, literary history would
furnish many an instance to prove that the
writer of fiction felt that a pleasant compliment had been paid him when his material was
made over by a writer for the stage.   Scott,
for example, aided Terry in adapting his
novels for theatrical performance ; and he did
this without any thought of reward.   But by
the time that Dickens succeeded Scott as the
most popular of English novelists the sentiment was changing. In " Nicholas Nickleby "
the author protested with acerbity against the
hack playwrights who made haste to put a
story on the stage even before its serial publication was finished.   His sense of injury was
sharpened by the clumsy disfiguring of his
work. Perhaps the injustice was never so
apparent as when a British playwright, one
Fitzball, captured Fenimore Cooper's " Pilot "
in 1826 and turned Long Tom Coffin into a
British sailor !—an act of piracy which a
recent historian of the London theatres, Mr.
H. B. Baker, records with hearty approval.

The possibility of an outrage like this still exists in England. In France, of course, the novelist has long had the exclusive right to adapt his own story to the stage ; and in the United States, also, he has it, if he gives notice formally on every copy of the book itself that he desires to reserve to himself the right of dramatization. But England has not as yet advanced thus far ; and no English author can make sure that he may not see a play ill-made out of his disfigured novel. Charles Reade protested in vain against unauthorized dramatization of his novels, and then, with characteristic inconsistency, made plays out of novels by Anthony Trollope and Mrs. Hodgson Burnett without asking their consent. But the unauthorized British adapter may not lawfully print the play he has compounded from a copyright novel, as any multiplication of copies would be an infringement of the copyright ; and Mrs. Hodgson Burnett succeeded in getting an injunction against an unauthorized dramatization of " Little Lord Fauntleroy " on proof that more than one copy of the unauthorized play had been made for use in the theatre. It is likely that one of the forthcoming modifications of the British law will be the extension to the novelist of the sole right to dramatize his own novel.

II.

From a consideration of the lengthening of the term of copyright and the development of certain subsidiary rights now acquired by an author, we come to a consideration of the next step in the process of evolution. This is the extension of an author's rights beyond the boundaries of the country of which he is a citizen, so that a book formally registered in one country shall by that single act and without further formality be protected from piracy [1] throughout the world. This great and needful improvement is now in course of accomplishment ; it is still far from complete, but year by year it advances farther and farther.

In the beginning the sovereign who granted a privilege, or at his caprice withheld it, could not, however strong his good-will, protect his subject's book beyond the borders of his realm ; and even when privilege broadened into copyright, a book duly registered was protected only within the State wherein the certificate was taken out. Very soon after Venice accorded the first privilege to John of

[1] "Piracy" is a term available for popular appeal but perhaps lacking in scientific precision. The present writer used it in a little pamphlet on "American Authors and British Pirates" rather by way of retort to English taunts. Yet the inexact use of the word indicates the tendency of public opinion.

Spira, the extension of the protection to the limits of a single State only was found to be a great disadvantage. Printing was invented when central Europe was divided and sub-divided into countless little states almost independent, but nominally bound together in the Holy Roman Empire. What is now the kingdom of Italy was cut up into more than a score of separate states, each with its own laws and its own executive. What is now the German Empire was then a disconnected medley of electorates, margravates, duchies, and grand-duchies, bishoprics and principalities, free towns and knight-fees, with no centre, no head, and no unity of thought or of feeling or of action. The printer-publisher made an obvious effort for wider protection when he begged and obtained a privilege not only from the authorities of the State in which he was working but also from other sovereigns. Thus, when the Florentine edition of the " Pandects " was issued in 1553, the publisher secured privileges in Florence first, and also in Spain, in the Two Sicilies, and in France. But privileges of this sort granted to non-residents were very infrequent, and no really efficacious protection for the books printed in another State was practically attainable in this way. Such protection, indeed, was wholly contrary to the spirit of the times, which held that an alien had no rights. In

France, for example, a ship wrecked on the coasts was seized by the feudal lord and retained as his, subject only to the salvage claim.[1]   In England a wreck belonged to the king unless a living being (man, dog, or cat) escaped alive from it ; and this claim of the crown to all the property of the unfortunate foreign owner of the lost ship was raised as late as 1771, when Lord Mansfield decided against it.   When aliens were thus rudely robbed of their tangible possessions, without public protest, there was not likely to be felt any keen sense of wrong at the appropriation of a possession so intangible as copyright.

What was needed was, first of all, an amelioration of the feeling toward aliens as such ; and second, such a federation of the petty states as would make a single copyright effective throughout a nation, and as would also make possible an international agreement for the reciprocal protection of literary property.   Only within the past hundred years or so, has this consolidation into compact and homogeneous nationalities taken place.   In the last century, for example, Ireland had its own laws, and Irish pirates reprinted at will books covered by English copyright.   In the preface to " Sir Charles Grandison," published in 1753, Richardson,

[1] A. C. Bernheim, "History of the Law of Aliens" (N. Y., 1885), p. 58.

novelist and printer, inveighed against the
piratical customs of the Hibernian publishers.
In Italy, what was published in Rome had
no protection in Naples or Florence. In
Germany, where Luther in his day had protested in vain against the reprinters, Goethe
and Schiller were able to make but little
money from their writings, as these were constantly pirated in the other German states,
and even imported into that in which they
were protected, to compete with the author's
edition. In 1826, Goethe announced a complete edition of his works, and, as a special
honour to the poet in his old age, " the
' Bundestag' undertook to secure him from
piracy in German cities." [1] With the union
of Ireland and Great Britain, with the accre-
tion about the kingdom of Sardinia of the
other provinces of Italy, with the compacting
of Germany under the hegemony of Prussia,
this inter-provincial piracy has wholly disappeared within the limits of these national
states.

The suppression of international piracy
passes through three phases. First, the nation
whose citizens are most often despoiled—and
this nation has nearly always been France—
endeavours to negotiate reciprocity treaties,
by which the writers of each of the contract-

[1] Lewes, " Life and Works of Goethe," p. 545.

ing countries may be enabled to take out copyrights in the other. Thus France had, prior to 1852, special treaties with Holland, Sardinia, Portugal, Hanover, and Great Britain. Secondly, a certain number of nations join in an international convention, extending to the citizens of all the copyright advantages that the citizens of each enjoy at home. Third, a State modifies its own local copyright law so as to remove the disability of the alien. This last step was taken by France in 1852 ; and in 1886 Belgium followed her example.

The French, seeking equity, are willing to do equity ; they ask no questions as to the nationality or residence of an author who offers a book for copyright ; and they do not demand reciprocity as a condition precedent. Time was when the chief complaint of French authors was against the Belgian reprinters ; but the Belgians, believing that the ship of state was ill-manned when she carried pirates in her crew, first made a treaty with France and then modified their local law into conformity with the French. These two nations, one of which was long the headquarters of piracy, now stand forward most honourably as the only two which really protect the full rights of an author.

Most of the states which had special copyright treaties one with another have adhered

to the convention of Berne, finally ratified in
1887.   Among them are France, Belgium,
Germany, Spain, Italy, Great Britain, and
Switzerland.   The adhesion of Austro-Hun-
gary, Holland, Norway, and Sweden is likely
not long to be delayed.   The result of this
convention is substantially to abolish the distinction between the subjects of the adhering
powers and to give to the authors of each
country the same faculty of copyright and of
stage-right that they enjoy at home, without
any annoying and expensive formalities of
registration or deposit in the foreign State.

The United States of America is now the
only one of the great powers of the world
which grants the protection of its laws to the
books of a friendly alien only when they are
manufactured in the United States.   From
having been one of the foremost states of the
world in the evolution of copyright, the United
States has now become one of the most backward,—even lagging behind Great Britain.
Nothing could be more striking than a contrast of the liberality with which the American
law treats the inventor and the niggardliness
with which it treats the author.

1890-1895.

THE DRAMATIZATION OF NOVELS.

FEW literary tasks seem easier of accomplishment than the making of a good
play out of a good novel. The playwright
has ready to his hand a story, a sequence of
situations, a group of characters artfully contrasted, the suggestion of the requisite scenery,
and occasional passages of appropriate conversation. What more is needed than a few
sheets of paper and a pair of scissors, a pen
and a little plodding patience? The pecuniary
reward is abundant; apparently the feat is
temptingly facile; and every year we see
many writers succumb to the temptation.
Whenever a novel hits the popular fancy and
is seen for a season in everybody's hands, be
it "Mr. Barnes of New York" or "She," "The
Quick or the Dead?" or "Robert Elsmere,"
the adapter steps forward and sets the story
on the stage, counting on the reflected reputation of the novel to attract the public to
witness the play. But the result of the calcu-
lation is rarely satisfactory, and the dramatized romance is rarely successful. Frequently

it is an instant failure, like the recent perver-
sion of " Robert Elsmere ; " occasionally it is
forced into a fleeting popularity by managerial
wiles, like the stage versions of " She " and
" Mr. Barnes of New York ; " and only now
and again is it really welcomed by the public,
like the dramatizations of " Little Lord
Fauntleroy " and " Uncle Tom's Cabin." So
it is that, if we look back along the lists of
plays which have had prolonged popularity,
we shall find the titles of very few dramatizations, and we shall discover that those which
chance to linger in our memory are recalled
chiefly because of a fortuitous association with
the fame of a favourite actor ; thus the semi-
operatic version of " Guy Mannering " brings
before us Charlotte Cushman's weird embodi-
ment of Meg Merrilies, just as the artless
adaptation of the " Gilded Age " evokes the
joyous humour of John T. Raymond as
Colonel Sellers. And if we were to make out
a list of novels which have been adapted to
the stage in the past thirty years or so, we
should discover a rarely broken record of
overwhelming disaster.

The reason of this is not far to seek. It is
to be found in the fundamental difference
between the art of the drama and the art of
prose-fiction—a difference which the adapter
has generally ignored or been ignorant of.
Perhaps it is not unfair to suggest that the

methods of the dramatist and of the novelist
are as unlike as the methods of the sculptor
and of the painter.   The difference between
the play and the novel is at bottom the difference between a precise and rigid form, and a
form of almost unlimited range and flexibility.
The drama has laws as unbending as those of
the sonnet, while the novel may extend itself
to the full license of an epic.   It is hardly too
much to say that nowadays the novelist has
complete freedom in choice of subject and in
method of treatment.   He may be concise or
he may be prolix.   He may lay the scene of
his story in a desert, and find his effect in the
slow analysis of a single human soul in awful
solitude ; or he may create a regiment of
characters which shall perform intricate evolu-
tions and move in serried ranks through the
crowded streets of a busy city.   He may riot
in the great phenomena of nature, forcing the
tornado, the gale at sea, the plunge of a
cataract, the purple sunset after a midsummer
storm, to create his catastrophe or to typify
some mood of his hero.   He may be a persis-
tent pessimist, believing that all is for the
worst in the worst of all possible worlds, and
painting his fellow-man in harsh black-and-
white, with a most moderate use of the white.
He may be a philosopher, using a thin veil of
fiction as a transparent mask for the exposition of his system of life.   He may adopt the

novel as a platform or as a pulpit; he may
use it as a means or he may accept it as an
end; he may do with it what he will; and if
he be a man to whom the world wishes to
listen or a man who has really something to
say, he gains a hearing.

In contrast with the license of the novelist
the limitations of the dramatist were never
more distinct than they are to-day. As the
playwright appeals to the playgoer, he is
confined to those subjects in which the broad
public can be interested and to the treatment
which the broad public will accept. While
the writer of romance may condense his work
into a short story of a column or two, or
expand it to a stout tome of a thousand pages,
the writer for the stage has no such choice;
his work must be bulky enough to last from
half-past eight to half-past ten at the shortest,
or at the longest from eight to eleven. In
the present condition of the theatre in Great
Britain and the United States, there is little
or no demand for the comedietta or for the
two-act comedy; a play must be long enough
and strong enough to furnish forth the whole
evening's entertainment. The dramatist may
divide his piece into three, or four, or five acts,
as he may prefer, but except from some good
and sufficient reason, there must be but a
single scene to each act. The characters
must be so many in number that no one shall

seem unduly obtrusive ; they must be sharply
contrasted ; most of them must be sympathetic to the spectators, for the audience in a
theatre, however pessimistic it may be indivi-
dually, is always optimistic as a whole. There
must be an infusion of humour at recurrent
intervals, and a slowly increasing intensity of
emotional stress. In short, the fetters of the
dramatist are as obvious as is the freedom of
the novelist.

Perhaps the chief disadvantage under which
the dramatist labours is that it is almost
impossible for him to show adequately the
progressive and wellnigh imperceptible disintegration of character under the attrition of
recurring circumstance. Time and space are
both beyond the control of the maker of plays,
while the story-teller may take his hero by
slow stages to the world's end. The drama
has but five acts at most, and the theatre is
but a few yards wide. Description is scarcely
permissible in a play ; and it may be the most
beautiful and valuable part of a novel. Comment by the author is absolutely impossible
on the stage ; and there are many who love
certain novels—Thackeray's for example—
chiefly because they feel therein the personal
presence of the author. It is at once the
merit and the difficulty of dramatic art that
the characters must reveal themselves ; they
must be illuminated from within, not from

without ; they must speak for themselves in
unmistakable terms ; and the author cannot
dissect them for us or lay bare their inner-
most thoughts with his pen as with a scalpel.
The drama must needs be synthetic, while
now the novel, more often than not, is analytic.
The vocabulary of the playwright must be
clear, succinct, precise, and picturesque, while
that of the novelist may be archaic, fantastic,
subtle, or allusive.   Simplicity and directness
are the ear-marks of a good play ; but we all
know good novels which are complex, invo-
lute, tortuous.   A French critic has declared
that the laws of the drama are Logic and
Movement, by which he means that in a good
play the subject clearly exposed at first moves
forward by regular steps, artfully prepared,
straight to its inevitable end.

After all, art is but a question of selection :
no man can put the whole of life either on the
stage or into a book.   He must choose the
facts which seem to him salient and which
will best serve his purpose.   He must reject
unhesitatingly all the others, as valuable in
themselves, it may be, but foreign to the work
in hand.   The principles differ which govern
this selection by the dramatist and by the
novelist.   Details which are insignificant in a
story may be of the greatest value in a play ;
and effects of prime importance in the tale
may be contrary to the practice of the play-

wright, or even physically impossible on the
stage. George Sand was a great novelist who
was passionately occupied with the theatre,
although she was wholly without the dramatic
gift; and in his biographical study of her
career and her character the late M. Caro
noted her constant failure as a dramatist, both
with original plays and with adaptations of her
own novels, declaring in these words the
reason of this failure: "What is needed on
the stage is the art of relief, the instinct of
perspective, adroitness of combination, and,
above all, action, again action, and always
action. It is natural and laughter-forcing
gayety, or the secret of powerful emotion, or
the unexpectedness which grips the attention "—all qualities which George Sand
lacked.

A mere sequence of *tableaux vivants*, even
if it include the characters and present the
situations of a successful tale, is not necessarily
a successful play, and certainly it is not a
good play. It is easy enough to scissor a
panorama of scenes from a story, but to make
over the story itself into a play is not so easy.
To get a true play out of a novel, the dramatist must translate the essential idea from the
terms of narrative into the terms of the drama.
He must disengage the fundamental subject
from the accidental incidents with which the
novelist has presented it. He must strip it to

the skeleton, and then he must clothe these bare bones with new flesh and fresh muscle in accordance with the needs of the theatre. He must disentangle the primary action and set this on the stage, clearly and simply. To do this it may be necessary to modify characters, to alter the sequence of scenes, to simplify motives, to condense, to clarify, to heighten. The more famous the novel—one might almost say the better the novel—the less likely is it to make a good play, because there is then a greater difficulty in disengaging the main theme from its subsidiary developments; and even when the playwright understands his trade, and realizes the gulf which yawns between the novel and the drama, the temptation to retain this fine scene of the story, or that delicately drawn character, or the other striking episode, is often too strong to be overcome, though he knows full well that these things are alien to the real play, as it ought to be. The playwright is conscious that the play-goers may look for these unessential scenes and characters and episodes, and he yields despite his judgment. Then in the end the play becomes a mere series of magic-lantern slides to illustrate the book; the real and the essential disappear behind the accidental and incidental; and the spectator cannot see the forest for the trees. The dramatizations of Scott, of Cooper, and of

Dickens, whatever their temporary popularity might be, and their immediate pecuniary success, were none of them good plays, nor were they ever wholly satisfactory to those who knew and loved the original novels. And Scott, Cooper, and Dickens are all sturdy and robust story-tellers, whose tales, one would think, might readily lend themselves to the freehand treatment and distemper illumination of the theatre. And "Uncle Tom's Cabin" has had much the same fate on the stage : the rough-hewn dramas made out of it have succeeded by no art of their own, but because of the overwhelming interest of the novel. I know of no stage version of Mrs. Stowe's story, or of any novel of Scott, of Cooper, or of Dickens, which has either organic unity or artistic symmetry.

The finer the novel, the more delicate and delightful its workmanship, the more subtle its psychology, the greater is the difficulty in dramatizing it, and the greater the ensuing disappointment. The frequent attempts to turn into a play "Vanity Fair" and the "Scarlet Letter" were all doomed to the certainty of failure, because the development of the central character and the leading motives, as we see them in the pages of the novelist, are not those by which they would best be revealed before the footlights. A true dramatist

might treat dramatically the chief figures of
Thackeray's novel or of Hawthorne's romance.
I can conceive a Becky Sharp play and
an Arthur Dimmesdale drama—the first a
comedy, with underlying emotion ; and the
second a tragedy, noble in its simple dignity ;
but neither of these possible plays would be
in any strict sense of the word dramatized
from the novel, although the germinant suggestion was derived from Thackeray and from
Hawthorne. They would be original plays,
independent in form, in treatment, and in
movement ; much as " All for Her " is an
original play by Messrs. Simpson and Meri-
vale, though it was obviously suggested by
the essential ideas of " Henry Esmond " and
" A Tale of Two Cities," which were adroitly
combined by two accomplished playwrights
feeling themselves at liberty to develop their
theme without any sense of responsibility to
the novelists. In like manner Mr. Boucicault's
admirably effective dramas, the " Colleen
Bawn " and the " Long Strike," are founded,
one on the " Collegians " of Gerald Griffin,
and the other on Mrs. Gaskell's " Mary
Barton ; " but the dramatist, while availing
himself freely of the novelist's labours, held
himself equally free to borrow from them no
more than he saw fit, and felt in nowise
bound to preserve in the play what did not
suit him in the story. I am told that the

foundation of Lord Lytton's " Richelieu " can be discovered in a romance by G. P. R. James ; and I have heard that a little story by Jules Sandeau was the exciting cause of MM. Sandeau and Augier's " Gendre de M. Poirier," the finest comedy of our century. At all times have playwrights been prone to take a ready-made myth. The great Greeks did it, using Homer as a quarry from which to get the rough blocks of marble needed for their heroic statues ; while Shakespeare and Molière found material for more than one piece in contemporary prose-fiction. But it would be absurd to consider any of these plays as a mere dramatization of a novel.

The difficulties and disadvantages of trying to make a play out of a popular tale, when the sequence and development of the story must be retained in the drama, are so distinctly recognized by novelists who happen also to be dramatists, that they are prone to stand aside and to leave the doubtful task to others. Dumas did not himself make a play out of his romantic tale, the "Corsican Brothers." And in the fall of 1887 there were produced in Paris two adaptations of successful novels which had been written by accomplished dramatists, " L'Abbé Constantin," by M. Ludovic Halévy, and " L'Affaire Clémenceau," by M. Alexandre Dumas *fils;* and in neither case did the dramatist adapt his own story. He knew better ; he knew that the good novel would not make a good play ; and while the novice rushed in where the expert feared to tread, the original author stood aside ready to take the profit, but not to run the risk.

I trust that I have not suggested that there are no novels which it is profitable or advisable to adapt to the stage. Such was not my intent, at least. What I wished to point out was that a panorama was not a play ; that to make a play out of a novel properly was a most difficult task ; and that the more widely popular the story, the less likely was the resultant piece to be valuable, because of the greater pressure to retain scenes foreign to the main theme as necessarily simplified and strengthened for the theatre.

Sometimes a story is readily set on the stage, because it was planned for the theatre before it appeared as a book. M. Georges Ohnet's "Serge Panine," for example, was first written as a play and afterwards as a novel, although the piece was not performed until after the story had achieved success. Charles Reade's "Peg Woffington" is avowedly founded on the comedy of "Masks and Faces," which Reade had written in collaboration with Tom Taylor, and of which it may seem to be a dramatization. Reade also found it easy to make an effective play out of his " Never

Too Late to Mend," because this novel was itself based on " Gold," an earlier piece of his.

Nor is this *ex-post-facto* dramatization the only possible or proper adaptation of a novel. A story of straightforward emotion may often be set on the stage to advantage, and with less alteration than is demanded by the more complex novel of character.   Stevenson declared that "a good serious play must be founded on one of the passionate *cruces* of life, where duty and inclination come nobly to the grapple ; and the same is true of what I call, for that reason, the dramatic novel." Now it is this dramatic novel, handling broadly a pregnant emotion, which can most often be dramatized successfully and satisfactorily.   And yet, even then, the story is perhaps best set on the stage by a playwright who has never read it.   This may sound like a paradox, but I can readily explain what I mean.   A well-known French piece, " Miss Multon," is obviously founded on the English novel " East Lynne."   I once asked M. Eugène Nus, one of the authors of " Miss Multon," how he came to adapt an English book ; and he laughingly answered that neither he nor his collaborator, M. Adolphe Bélot, had ever read " East Lynne."   At a pause during a rehearsal of another play of theirs, an actress had told M. Bélot that she had just finished a

story which would make an excellent play,
and thereupon she gave him the plot of Mrs.
Wood's novel.   And the plot, the primary
suggestion, the first nucleus of situation and
character, this is all these dramatists needed ;
and in most cases it is all that any dramatist
ought to borrow from any novelist.   It is thus
that we may account in part for the merit of
Mr. Pinero's play " The Squire," which is perhaps more or less remotely derived from Mr.
Hardy's " Far from the Madding Crowd."
Not to have read the story he is to dramatize
is, however, a privilege possible to but few
playwrights.

The next best thing is to have the needful
power to disengage the main theme of the
story and to be able to reincarnate this in a
dramatic body.   A good example may be
seen in " Esmeralda," the comedy which Mr.
William Gillette helped Mrs. Burnett to make
out of a tale of hers.   But this has been done
so rarely on the English-speaking stage that
I must perforce seek other examples in France.
As it happens I can name three plays, all
founded on novels, all adapted to the stage
by the novelist himself, and all really superior to the novels from which they were
taken.   Jules Sandeau's " Mademoiselle de la
Seiglière " is a pretty tale, but the comedy
which the late eminent comedian, M. Regnier,
of the Comédie-Française, aided M. Sandeau

to found upon it is far finer as a work of literature.   "Le Marquis de Villemer" of George Sand is a lovely novel, but it lacks the firmness, the force, and the symmetry to be found in the play which M. Alexandre Dumas *fils* helped her to construct from it, and which, therefore, won the popular favour denied to most of her other dramatic attempts. And in like manner M. Dumas himself re-composed his "Dame aux Camélias," and made a moving novel into one of the most moving plays of our time.   In all three cases the drama is widely different from the story, and the many needful modifications have been made with marvellous technical skill. Hardly any more profitable investigation could be suggested to the 'prentice play-wright than first to read one of these novels, and then to compare it faithfully with the play which its author evolved from it ; and the student of the physics of play-making could have no better laboratory work than to think out the reasons for every change.

Such a student will discover, for instance, that the dramatist cannot avail himself of one of the most effective devices of the nove-list, who may keep a secret from his readers, which is either revealed to them unexpectedly and all at once, or which they are allowed to solve for themselves from chance hints skil-fully let fall in the course of the narrative.

But the dramatist knows that to keep a secret from the spectator for the sake of a single, sudden surprise is to sacrifice to one little and temporary shock of discovery the cumulative force of a heroic struggle against a foreseen catastrophe. To take an example from one of the most accomplished of Greek playwrights, the strife against awakening doubt, the wrestling with a growing conviction, the agony of final knowledge which we see in " Œdipus," and the indisputable effect these have on us, are the result of not keeping a secret. The great play of Sophocles has the interest of expectation, though every spectator might foresee and foretell the outcome of the opening situations. True dramatic interest is aroused, not by deceiving or disappointing the audience as to the end to be reached, or even by keeping it unduly in doubt as to this, but by choosing the least commonplace and most effective means of reaching that end. And true dramatic interest is sustained, not by a vulgar surprise, but by exciting the sympathy of the spectator for the character immeshed in dangers which the audience comprehend clearly—by exciting the sympathy of the spectator so that he becomes the accomplice of the playwright, putting himself in the place of the persons of the play, and feeling with them as the dread catastrophe draws nigh.

The novelist may play tricks with his readers, because he knows that they can take time to think if they are in doubt, and can even turn back a chapter or two to straighten out the sequence of events. But the dramatist knows that the spectators have no time for retrospection and for piecing together, and therefore he is not warranted in leaving them in the dark for a minute. And it is this total divergence of principle that so many novelists, and so many of those who attempt to drama- tize novels, absolutely fail to apprehend. In her needless biography of Richard Brinsley Sheridan, Mrs. Oliphant found fault with the screen scene of the "School for Scandal" because we see Lady Teazle conceal herself. "It would, no doubt," she wrote, "have been higher art could the dramatist have deceived his audience as well as the personages of the play, and made us also parties in the surprise of the discovery." This criticism is simply a master-stroke of dramatic incompetence, and it is astounding that any one able to read and write could consider that most marvel- lous specimen of dramatic construction, the screen scene of the "School for Scandal," without seeing that the whole effect of the situation, and half the force of the things said and done by the characters on the stage, would be lost if we did not know that Lady Teazle was in hiding within hearing of Joseph's impotent explanations, of Charles's careless gayety, and of Sir Peter's kindly thoughtfulness.

In a play there must be as little as possible of either confusion or doubt. As the French critic said, the laws of the drama are Logic and Movement—logic in the exposition and sequence of events, movement in the emotions presented. And here we come to another dissimilarity of the drama from prose-fiction— the need of more careful and elaborate structure in a play. A novel a man may make up as he goes along haphazard, but in a play the last word must be thought out before the first word is written. The plot must move forward unhesitatingly to its inevitable conclusion. There can be no wavering, no faltering, no lingering by the wayside. And every effect, every turn of the story must be prepared adroitly and unostentatiously. M. Legouvé calls the play-goer both exacting and inconsistent, in that he insists that everything which passes before him on the stage shall be at once foretold and unforeseen. The play-goer is shocked if anything drops from the clouds unexpected, yet he is bored if anything is unduly announced. The dramatist must now and again take the play-goers into his confidence by a chance word to which they pay no attention at the time, so that when the situation abruptly turns on itself, they say to themselves, "Why, of course, he warned us of that. What fools we were not to guess what was coming!" And then they are delighted.

In considering Lord Tennyson's "Queen Mary" when it first appeared, Mr. Henry James remarked that the " fine thing in a real drama is that, more than any other work of lite- rary art, it needs a masterly structure, a process which makes a demand upon an artist's rarest gifts." And then Mr. James compressed a chapter of criticism into a figure of speech. " The five-act drama," he said, " serious or humorous, poetic or prosaic, is like a box of fixed dimensions and inelastic material, into which a mass of precious things are to be packed away. . . . The precious things seem out of all proportion to the compass of the receptacle ; but the artist has an assurance that with patience and skill a place may be made for each, and that nothing need be clipped or crimped, squeezed or damaged." It is this infinite patience and this surpassing skill that the ordinary theatrical adapter of a novel is wholly without. He does not acknow- ledge the duties of the dramatist, and he is hardly conscious even that a play is a work of literary art. Few of those who try to write for the stage, without having penetrated the secret of the drama, realize the indisputable necessity of the preliminary plan. They do

not suspect that a play must needs be built
as carefully and as elaborately as a cathedral,
in which not only the broad nave and the
massive towers but every airy pinnacle and
every flying buttress contribute to the total
effect. As the architect, who is primarily an
artist, must do his work in full accord with
the needs of the civil engineer who understands the mechanics of building, so the
dramatist, who deals with human character
and human passion, is guided in his labour by
the precepts and practice of the mere play-
maker, the expert who is master of the
mechanics of the stage. The accomplished
architect is his own civil engineer, and the
true dramatist is a playwright also, a man
fully conversant with the possibilities of the
theatre and fully recognizing its limitations.
"To work successfully beneath a few grave,
rigid laws," said Mr. James in the criticism
from which I have already quoted, "is always
a strong man's highest ideal of success." This
serves to explain why the sonnet with its
inexorable rules has been ever a favourite
with great poets, and why the drama with its
metes and bounds has always had a fascination
for the literary artist.

Some of the limitations of the drama are
inherent in the form itself, and are therefore
immutable and permanent. Some are ex-
ternal, and are therefore temporary and vari-

able. For example, it has always seemed to
me that inadequate attention has been given
to the influence exerted on dramatic literature
by the size of the theatre and by the circumstances of the performance. This influence
was most potent in shaping the Greek drama,
the Elizabethan plays of England, and the
French tragedy under Louis XIV. The un-
adorned directness of Æschylus impresses us
mightily ; the same massive breadth of treatment we find also, although in a minor degree,
in Sophocles and Euripides ; on all three
dramatists it was imposed by the physical
conditions of the theatre. Their plays were
to be performed out of doors, by actors speaking through a resonant mouthpiece in a huge
mask, and lifted on high shoes so that they
might be seen by thousands of spectators
from all classes of the people. Of necessity
the dramatist chose for his subject a familiar
tale, and gave it the utmost simplicity of plot
while he sought a gradually increasing intensity of emotion. The movement of his story
must needs be slow ; there was no change of
scene, and there was no violence of action.
Thus it happens that the impassible dignity
of the Greek drama was due, not wholly to
the æsthetic principles of Greek art, but to
the physical conditions of the Greek theatre.
The so-called rule of the three unities—the
rule that a play should show but *one* action in

one place and in *one* day, a rule that later
critics deduced from the practice of the Greeks
—was not consciously obeyed by Æschylus,
Sophocles, or Euripides, although the most of
their plays seem to fall within it, simply from
force of circumstances.

As different as may be were the large and
splendid open-air representations of these
great Greek dramas before the assembled
citizens of a Greek state, and the cramped and
dingy performances of Shakespeare's plays in
the rude theatre of Queen Elizabeth's day,
when the stage was but a small platform set
up at one end of the half-roofed courtyard of
an inn. Then there was but a handful of
spectators, standing thickly in the pit or seated
in the shallow galleries close to the actors.
The stage was unencumbered with scenery,
and author and actors felt themselves free to
fill it with movement ; and so the plays of
that time abound in murders and trials, in
councils and in battles. The audience had
perforce to imagine the background of the
story, and so the authors did not hesitate to
change the scene with careless frequency. As
the noble marble theatres of Greece imposed
on the dramatist an equal severity, so the
mean, half-timbered playhouses of Elizabethan
England warranted the noisy violence and
the rushing eloquence and the fiery poesy
which seem to us to-day chief among the

characteristics of the dramatic literature of
that epoch.

Crossing the Channel to France, we find that
the decorum and pseudo-dignity of tragedy
under Louis XIV. are due, in part at least, to
the court plumes and velvet coats which the
actors wore even when personating the noblest
of Romans or the simplest of Greeks ; and
also to the fact that the stage was circum-
scribed by a double row of benches occupied
by the courtiers.   Through the ranks of these
fine gentlemen, coming and going at their
will, and chatting together freely, the Cid and
Phèdre had to make their way to a small
central space where they might stand stock-
still to declaim.   Swift motion and even vigorous gesture were impossible.   The wily Racine
found his account in substituting a subtle self-
analytic and concentrated psychologic action
for purely physical movement, a choice con-
sonant to his genius.   On the production of
Voltaire's " Sémiramis," it is recorded that an
usher had to break through the ring of spectators seated and standing on the stage, with a
plaintive appeal that they would make way
for the ghost of Ninus.   Under conditions like
these it is no wonder that in time French
tragedy stiffened into a parody of itself.

The physical conditions of the stage are
different in every time and in every place ;
they are continually changing ; but the true

dramatist makes his work conform to them,
consciously or unconsciously. The poet who
is not a true dramatist seeks to model a
modern drama on an ancient—a fundamental
and fatal defect. The attempt of Voltaire to
imitate Sophocles was foredoomed to failure.
The endeavour of many later English poets
to use the Shakespearean formula is equally
futile. Mr. Stedman has shrewdly pointed
out that Tennyson's " Queen Mary " differs
from the work of the Elizabethan dramatist
in that it is the result of a " forced effort, while
the models after which it is shaped were in
their day an intuitive form of expression."

This forced effort is really due to a mis-
understanding of the older dramatists. If
Sophocles had lived in the days of Voltaire,
he would have written in accordance with the
physical conditions of the French theatre of
that era. If Shakespeare had lived in the
days of Æschylus, he would have produced
Greek plays of the most sublime simplicity.
Were he alive now, we may be sure that he
would not construct a piece in mimicry of the
Elizabethan dramatists, as Lord Tennyson
chose to do. He would use the most modern
form : and, incomparable craftsman as he was,
he would bend to his bidding every modern
improvement—music, costume, scenery, and
lighting. Were Cæsar and Napoleon men of our
time, they would not now fight with the short

sword or the flint-lock, but with the Winchester and the Gatling.

This, I take it, is one of the chief characteristics of the true dramatist—that he sees at once when a form is outworn, and lets the dead past bury its dead; that he utilizes all the latest devices of the stage, while recognizing frankly and fully the limitations imposed by the physical conditions of the theatre. As I have already suggested, these limitations forbid not a few of the effects permissible to the novelist. No dramatist may open his story with a solitary horseman, as was once the fashion of fiction; nor can he show the hero casually rescuing the heroine from a prairie on fire, or from a slip into the rapids of Niagara; and he finds it impossible to get rid of the villain by throwing him under the wheels of a locomotive. Not only is the utilization of the forces of nature very difficult on the stage, and extremely doubtful, but the description of nature herself is out of place; and however expert the scene-painter, he cannot hope to vie with Victor Hugo or Hawthorne in calling up before the eye the grandeur or the picturesqueness of the scene where the action of the story comes to its climax.

Time was when the drama was first, and prose-fiction limped a long way after; time was when the novelists, even the greatest of

them, began as playwrights. Cervantes, Le
Sage, Fielding, all studied the art of character-
drawing on the boards of a theatre, although
no one of their plays keeps the stage to-day,
while we still read with undiminished zest the
humorous record of the adventures and misad-
ventures of Don Quixote, Gil Blas, and Tom
Jones. Scott was, perhaps, the first great
novelist who did not learn his trade behind
the scenes. It seemed to Lowell that before
Fielding " real life formed rather the scenic
background than the substance, and that the
characters are, after all, merely players who
represent certain types rather than the living
types themselves." It may be suggested that
the earlier novels reflected the easy expedients
and artificial manners of the theatre, much as
the writers may have employed the processes
of the stage. Since Fielding and Scott the
novel has been expanding, until it seeks to
overshadow its elder brother. The old inter-
dependence of the drama and prose-fiction
has ceased ; nowadays the novel and the play
are independent, each with its own aims and
its own methods.

While, on the one hand, there are not
lacking those who see in the modern novel
but a bastard epic in low prose, so there are
not wanting others, novelists and critics of
literature, chiefly in France, where the principles of dramatic art are better understood

than elsewhere, who are so impressed by the number and magnitude of the restrictions which bind the dramatist, that they are inclined to declare the drama itself to be an outworn form. They think that the limitations imposed on the dramatist are so rigid that first-rate literary workmen will not accept them, and that first-rate literary work cannot be hoped for. These critics are on the verge of hinting that nowadays the drama is little more than a polite amusement, just as others might call oratory now little more than the art of making after-dinner speeches. They suggest that the play is sadly primitive when compared with the perfected novel of the nineteenth century. They remark that the drama can show but a corner of life, while prose-fiction may reveal almost the whole of it. They assert boldly that the drama is no longer the form of literature best suited to the treatment of the subjects in which the thinking people of to-day are interested. They declare that the novelist may grapple resolutely with a topic of the times, though the dramatist dare not scorch his fingers with a burning question. The Goncourts, in the preface of their undramatic play, "La Patrie en Danger," announced that "the drama of to-day is not literature."

It is well to mass these criticisms together that they may be met once and for all. It is

true that the taste for analysis which dominates the prose-fiction of our time has affected
the drama but little ; and it is not easy to
say whether or not the formulas of the theatre
can be so enlarged, modified, and made more
delicate that the dramatist can really rival
the novelist in psychologic subtlety. Of
course, if the novel continues to develop in
one direction in accordance with a general
current of literature, and if the drama does
not develop along the same lines, then the
drama will be left behind, and it will become
a mere sport, an empty spectacle, a toy for
children, spoonmeat for babes.

A book, however fine or peculiar, delicate
or spiritual, goes in time to the hundred or
the thousand congenial spirits for whom it
was intended ; it may not get to its address
at once or even in its author's life-time ; but
sooner or later its message is delivered to all
who are ready to receive it. A play can have
no such fate ; and for it there is no redemp-
tion, if once it is damned. It cannot live by
pleasing a few only ; to earn the right to
exist, it must please the many. And this is
at the bottom of all dislike for the dramatic
form—that it appeals to the crowd, to the
broad public, to all classes alike, rich and
poor, learned and ignorant, rough and refined.
And this is to me the great merit of the
drama, that it cannot be dilettante, finikin,

precious, narrow. It must handle broad
themes broadly. It must deal with the common facts of humanity. It is the democrat
of literature. Théophile Gautier, who disliked the theatre, said that an idea never
found its way on the stage until it was worn
threadbare in newspapers and in novels. And
he was not far out. As the drama appeals to
the public at large, it must consider seriously
only those subjects which the public at large
can understand and are interested in. There
are exceptions, no doubt, now and again,
when an adroit dramatist succeeds in captivating the public with a theme still in de-
bate. M. Sardou, for example, wrote " Daniel
Rochat " ten years before Mrs. Ward wrote
" Robert Elsmere," and the Frenchman's play
was acted in New York for more than a
hundred nights. M. Alexandre Dumas *fils*
has again and again discussed on the stage
marriage and divorce and other problems that
vex mankind to-day. And in Scandinavia,
Henrik Ibsen, a dramatist of exceeding technical skill and abundant ethical vigour, has
brought out a series of dramas (many of them
successful on the stage), of which the most
important is " Ghosts," wherein he considers
with awful moral force the doctrine of here-
dity, proving by example that the sins of the
fathers are visited on the children. With
instances like these in our memories, we may

suggest that the literary deficiencies of the
drama are not in the form, but in the inex-
pertness or inertness of the dramatists of the
day.   There are few of the corner-stone facts
of human life, and there are none of the
crucible-tried passions of human character,
which the drama cannot discuss quite as well
as the novel.

Indeed, the drama is really the noblest
form of literature, because it is the most direct.
It calls forth the highest of literary faculties
in the highest degree—the creation of character, standing firm on its own feet, and
speaking for itself.   The person in a play
must *be* and *do*, and the spectator must see
what he is, and what he does, and why.
There is no narrator standing by to act as
chorus, and there needs none.   If the dramatist know his trade, if he have the gift of the
born playwright, if his play is well made, then
there is no call for explanation or analysis, no
necessity of dissecting or refining, no demand
for comment or sermon, no desire that any
one palliate or denounce what all have seen.
Actions speak louder than words.   That this
direct dramatic method is fine enough for the
most abstruse intellectual self-questioning
when the subject calls for this, and that in
the mighty hand of genius it is capable of
throwing light in the darkest corners and
crannies of the tortured and tortuous human

soul, ought not to be denied by any one who may have seen on the stage the "Œdipus" of Sophocles, the "Hamlet" of Shakespeare, the "Misanthrope" of Molière, or the "Faust" of Goethe.

1889.

ON CERTAIN PARALLELISMS BETWEEN THE ANCIENT AND THE MODERN DRAMA.

FOR the man of letters who has let his classical studies lapse on leaving college, and who takes them up again a score of years later, there are compensations, as I have recently discovered by personal experience. What the man of letters who does this has lost is incalculable and irrecoverable, no doubt, and what he may gain is but little indeed and of small worth,—yet it is something if it be only a renewed freshness of view. And it is indisputable that this is the chief gain,—this ability to look at old texts from new standpoints, and to interpret the life and the literature of the past by the aid of a deeper knowledge of the life and the literature of the present.

The vital principles of any art are always the same, and they subsist through the ages essentially unchanged, however much they may seem to be modified superficially by the

varying fashions of succeeding generations.
Of no art are the fundamental laws more
absolutely fixed than are those of the drama.
When, therefore, one who has given his attention for twenty-five years to the modern
stage returns to the study of the ancient
theatre, he might fairly be expected now and
again to note points of contact between the
old and the new.

A knowledge of the manners and customs
of the players and the playwrights of Paris
and London and New York enables the
student to understand better than he could
otherwise the manners and the customs of
the players and the playwrights of Athens
and Rome. When anyone having an acquaintance with the modern playhouse in-
quires into the practices of the ancient
theatre, he cannot but remark, in the older
plays, features which are often supposed to be
the sole property of the most recent playwrights. In the Greek theatre, for instance,
it is not difficult to discover that the dramatist was generally careful to provide an "exit-
speech" whenever an important character left
the stage ; nor is it hard to detect among the
plays of Euripides more than one specimen
of the "star-piece." Though there may be
no Greek equivalents for these technical
terms, the things these words denote existed
in Greece none the less.

F

The terminology of the contemporary theatre is precise and copious, although it has not as yet been recorded fully in any dictionary of the English language, or even in any technical vocabulary of its own. A " star-piece," for example, is a play so devised as to display all the histrionic powers of the performer of the chief part. Certain of Shakespeare's plays are obviously " star-pieces : " " Hamlet," for one, and " Richard III." for another ; and so is the " Medea " of Euripides. Medea is not only the " star-part," but the other characters of the play are little more than mere " feeders,"—that is to say, they exist, not for their own sake, but solely for their relation to Medea ; and they speak, not to reveal themselves, but solely to afford occasion to Medea to express herself fully and at length and under the strain of the most poignant emotions. The character played by the protagonist is all-important, and the characters played by the deuteragonist and by the tritagonist are all of them subordinated and effaced. It is known that there were strolling companies of performers in Greece and in the Grecian colonies, as there have been of late years in Great Britain and the United States (Haigh's " Attic Theatre," p. 43) ; and to give a fairly satisfactory performance of the " Medea," only one great actor was needed.

A renowned Athenian protagonist could "go on the road" with the "Medea," as certain of pleasing the multitudes who would flock to see him act in the theatres of the smaller Greek cities, as Madame Sarah Bernhardt is now certain to delight the audiences who fill the playhouses of all the larger towns of the whole world to behold her suffer and die in "La Tosca." Nor has M. Sardou contrived "La Tosca" more adroitly for this special portability than Euripides composed the "Medea." Euripides is like M. Sardou in more ways than one; in his exceeding cleverness, for instance, in his dramaturgic dexterity, in his mastery of theatrical device, in his predilection for women as his chief characters.

"It is stated," so Mr. Haigh reminds us in his admirable volume on the "Attic Theatre" (p. 76), citing the authorities for the statement, "that Sophocles was accustomed to write his plays with a view to the capacities of his actors." No one who has investigated the methods of the great modern dramatists would venture to dispute this assertion; and it would be easy to adduce reasons for thinking that Euripides did what Sophocles was accused of doing.[1] An analysis of the "Medea" has convinced me that in composing this play, Euripides was, in all pro-

[1] Compare Aristotle, "Poetics," 9 (1451 b 38).

bability, carefully " fitting " — to use the
technical term of the theatre of to-day—some
Athenian actor by whose extraordinary histrionic ability he wished to profit, just as
M. Sardou, in composing " La Tosca," fitted
Madame Sarah Bernhardt, just as Molière,
for that matter, certainly fitted Mademoiselle de Molière when he was writing " Le
Misanthrope," and just as Shakespeare possibly fitted Master Burbage when he was
writing " Hamlet." And while " Hamlet "
and " Le Misanthrope " are the masterpieces
of their authors, the " Medea " again is rather
like " La Tosca," in that it owes its permanent
popularity to the histrionic opportunities it
affords. After all, what we go to the theatre
to see is — in the final analysis — acting.
Whatever we may like in the library, in the
theatre we prefer the plays which give most
scope to the actors.

"Exit-speech " is the name given to the
final words spoken by a character before he
leaves the stage after an important scene.
Nowadays, an exit-speech is generally a
point of one kind or another, rhetorical or
jocular. In Shakespeare's time, the exit-
speech frequently ended with a couplet, the
rhymes of which were signals to the ground-
lings to be ready with their applause. In the
great period of the Spanish drama which was
contemporary with the Elizabethan drama of

England, the utility of the exit-speech was perfectly understood, and in the " Arte nuevo de hacer comedias " in which Lope de Vega laid down precepts for the guidance of practical dramatists, he advises the 'prentice playwright thus :

"Adorn the end of your scenes with some swelling phrase, with some joke, with lines more carefully polished, so that the actor at his exit does not leave the audience in ill-humour."

In the Greek drama the exit-speech is frequent. In the "Medea," again, Jason's final words at the end of the stormy scene with his wife, have all the characteristics of the "exit-speech" (619-22):

ἀλλ' οὖν ἐγὼ μὲν δαίμονας μαρτύρομαι,
ὡς πάνθ' ὑπουργεῖν σοί τε καὶ τέκνοις θέλω·
σοὶ δ' οὐκ ἀρέσκει τἀγάθ', ἀλλ' αὐθαδίᾳ
φίλους ἀπωθεῖ· τοιγὰρ ἀλγυνεῖ πλέον.

An exit-speech also of the most approved type is Medea's, when she leaves the stage after the marvellously pathetic scene with her children, and after the messenger has declared the success of her scheme to kill her rival (1244-50):

ἄγ' ὦ τάλαινα χεὶρ ἐμὴ, λαβὲ ξίφος,
λάβ', ἕρπε πρὸς βαλβῖδα λυπηρὰν βίου,
καὶ μὴ κακισθῇς, μηδ' ἀναμνησθῇς τέκνων
ὡς φίλταθ', ὡς ἔτικτες· ἀλλὰ τήνδε γε

λαθοῦ βραχεῖαν ἡμέραν παίδων σέθεν,
κᾆπειτα θρήνει· καὶ γὰρ εἰ κτενεῖς σφ' ὅμως
φίλοι γ' ἔφυσαν, δυστυχὴς δ' ἐγὼ γυνή.

The complement of the exit-speech is
the device now known as "working up an
entrance." A leading actor likes to have his
coming before the audience for the first time
in the play carefully prepared and plainly
announced, so that expectancy may be aroused
and recognition may follow at once upon his
appearance on the stage. Every playgoer can
recall instances of the ingenuity with which
the modern playwrights have been able to
work up the entrance of important characters ;
there is no better example, perhaps, than the
first appearance of the heroine in "Adrienne
Lecouvreur," the drama devised for Rachel by
Scribe and M. Legouvé. Now this working
up an entrance for the chief persons of the
play, was far more needful in the Greece of
old than it is in the Paris and in the New
York of to-day, for the Grecian theatres were
many times the size of ours, and the actors
wore masks which hid their features, and—so
far as I know, at least—there were no pro-
grammes to aid in identification. Therefore,
we find that the Greek dramatists were very
careful to work up the entrance even of
unimportant characters. In the "Medea,"
once more, after the prologue in which the
nurse declares herself, no person of the play

comes on unannounced by some one already on the stage ; and the appearance of Medea herself is worked up quite in the most modern manner, her loud bewailings off the stage being expounded by the nurse.

The fact is that the psychology of the theatrical spectator is very much the same in all climes and in all ages. The New York boy who perches in the upper gallery of the Broadway Theatre, however deficient in intelligence when compared with the citizen of Athens seated on a marble bench in the beautiful theatre of Dionysus, has needs like his in so far as they are both playgoers. Both demand clearness above all things ; both desire not to be left in doubt as to what is going on before them. For a man at the play, understanding is the condition precedent of enjoyment.

It is greatly to be desired that some classical scholar should familiarize himself with the modern theatre, so that he might approach the study of the drama of antiquity with a full understanding of the present methods of the same art. Much of the value of Patin's " Tragiques Grecs " is due to his knowledge of the French theatre and to his constant use of the modern stage for comparison with the ancient. In this, as in other respects, Professor Mahaffy has followed in Patin's footsteps. But no one has yet done for the Greeks what the late M. Goumy attempted to do for the

Latins—to explain the past in terms of the present. It would be too much to say that M. Goumy, who died before he had half finished his task, was wholly successful in finding modern equivalents for ancient experiences. But " Les Latins " is a volume to be read with refreshment and stimulation, and it is good for us to be told that Cæsar's " Commentaries " was really what we Americans might call " a campaign autobiography," and that Cicero did not deliver his orations as they have come down to us, but " asked leave to print," so to speak, that he might polish his periods at leisure.

Though I have neither the sholarship nor the time to undertake the explanation of the ancient drama by the modern theatre in the method I have suggested, I can furnish a few additional instances of parallelism perhaps not unworthy of record. The likeness of the Greek tragedy, with its appropriate music, its slow and stately movement, and its use of local legend, to the Wagnerian music-drama has been dwelt on sufficiently ; and, even as I pen these paragraphs, I find in the second number of the new "Revue de Paris " an essay on the specific resemblances of "Die Walküre " to the " Antigone." But less attention has been drawn to a more recent return to Greek principles of playmaking, Ibsen's presentation of only the culminating point of the plot, and

his concentration of all the interest of the
action into its compact climax, in which the
" Œdipus Rex " itself is scarcely more skilfully
contrived than is " Ghosts."

It may seem most irreverent to suggest a
similarity between a masterpiece of humour
like the " Frogs " and an amusing modern
burlesque like the " Adonis," in which Mr.
Dixey parodied the peculiarities of Mr. Henry
Irving, much as some Athenian comedian
must have mimicked the mannerisms of
Euripides, but nevertheless the similarity of
the two pieces is striking enough. Indeed,
the difference between " Adonis " and the
" Frogs " is due mainly to the fact that the
author of " Adonis " was only a clever comic
playwright, while the author of the " Frogs "
happened also to be a great poet—just as it
is also his poetic power which gives Euripides
his immeasurable superiority over M. Sardou.
In the " Frogs," for example, Bacchus, in the
costume of Hercules, is like a modern actor in
classic attire, crowned with the very latest
style of stove-pipe hat ; and when Bacchus
appeals to his priest sitting officially in front
of the stage, he is not unlike the comedian of
our time who holds a colloquy with the leader
of the band. I confess that the comic servant,
Xanthias, in the " Frogs," complaining that he
is not allowed to complain, reminds me of the
comic servant, Greppo, in the " Black Crook,"

also involved in mysterious adventures which
he does not understand.

I wonder whether or not it was a tradition
of the Grecian theatres that the performer
who played Xanthias, or any other comic servant of the sort, should wear many garments
of contrasting colours, superimposed one on
the other so that he might excite the laughter
of unthinking spectators by removing them
one by one. This "business" is traditional
with the Second Grave Digger in the "Hamlet"
of Shakespeare, and with Jodelet in the " Pré-
cieuses Ridicules" of Molière; and it is derived
probably from some forgotten farce of the
Middle Ages, which in turn was possibly descended from some Roman pantomime. Visible
jests of this kind are very long-lived, and no
doubt many of them passed over from the
Latin *fabulæ Atellanæ* to the Italian *commedie
dell' arte.*

For the adapted comedies of Plautus and
Terence, with abundant Roman allusions
flowering out of Grecian plots, more or less
skilfully transplanted, there are many modern
parallels. It is not at all uncommon to see
on the modern English - speaking stage a
French or a German play, roughly twisted
into conformity with the conditions of British
or American life. They may be amusing, like
Mr. Augustin Daly's later adaptations from
the German, or they may be exciting like some

of his earlier adaptations from the French;
yet there cannot but be always an obvious
and inevitable unreality in any drama merely
decanted in this fashion. While the comedies
of Plautus may thus be likened, not unfairly, to the modern English localized arrange-
ments of foreign plays, the skill with which
the Latin dramatist presented the every-day
life of the Roman household and market-place
suggests that his comedies may also be compared with the amusing and broadly sketched
pieces in which Mr. Harrigan has most amus-
ingly set before us the characteristics of the
polyglot population of New York.

Perhaps no peculiarity of Greek comedy
has seemed stranger to latterday commentators than the parabasis; and yet to discover
modern equivalents even for this is not difficult. I think it is even possible to derive from
our own experience the reason why the earlier
dramatists were moved to make use of this
device. The parabasis—so Müller describes
it in the " History of the Literature of Ancient
Greece " (i. p. 401)—is " an address of the
chorus in the middle of the comedy"; and in
it " the poet makes his chorus speak of his
own poetical affairs, of the object and end of
his productions, of his services to the state,
of his relation to his rivals, and so forth."
Then the chorus sings a lyrical poem, and
recites in trochaic verse " some joking com-

plaint, some reproach against the city, some
witty sally against the people." It is this
second part of the parabasis that Professor
Mahaffy, in his " History of Greek Literature "
(i. chap. xx.) likens to the "topical song" of
the modern burlesque, " which is always composed on current events, and has verses added
from week to week, as new points of public
interest crop up."

The first part of the parabasis, wherein the
poet makes the chorus his own mouthpiece,
and addresses the audience almost in his own
person, is very closely akin to the Elizabethan
prologue, in which the dramatist discussed
the play about to be performed, in which
occasionally he abused his rivals, and in which
he sometimes vaunted himself. And here the
prologue, like the parabasis, performed a useful
function ; for as the psychology of the playgoer
changes but little through the ages, so also
the psychology of the playwright is substantially the same in Periclean Athens and
in Elizabethan London. Above all things,
the spectator wants to be able to understand
what he is seeing, and the dramatist wishes to
have his work seen from his own point of
view. The playwright is glad to have the
right of rising to a personal explanation.
Nowadays the novelist and the poet can declare in a preface the code by which they wish
to be judged. The dramatist cannot avail

himself of this privilege ; and the prologue or
the parabasis is the only preface he is permitted. If he cannot get the ear of the public
for an explanation outside of his work, he
must perforce make this explanation a part of
the work itself, placing it either at the beginning, as Ben Jonson did, or in the middle, as
did Aristophanes.

The frequency with which the prologue was
made to perform this function is well brought
out in " A Study of the Prologue and Epilogue
in English Literature " (by " G. S. B.," London,
1884), wherein it is shown that the prologue
was of real service to Ben Jonson, and that it
was useful even to Dryden, although he had
already other means of reaching the public
ear.   The prologue and the epilogue still
accompanied new plays at the end of the last
century, although they had ceased to have
any close connection with the pieces before
and after which they were spoken.   It is
obvious that the prologue and epilogue in
Sheridan's plays, for example, are mere survivals of an outworn fashion.

Yet even in this century, when the dramatist
can call on the journalists to publish abroad
any declaration he may desire to make, there
are occasions when the temptation to expound
his own theories of his art inside the work of
art itself are too strong to be overcome.   In
the " Antony " of the elder Dumas, in the

fourth act, there is a discussion between
Eugène and the Baron de Marsane about
Romanticism,—what is this but a prose parabasis cut into dialogue? And in the " Denise "
of the younger Dumas, the analysis of the
thesis of the piece by Thouvenin,—in what
manner does this differ essentially from the
parabasis? So frequent has been the use of a
character like Thouvenin by M. Dumas *fils*,
and by certain of his contemporaries, that the
French critics have been forced to find a name
for this new stage-type ; they call the character
who explains the play a *raisonneur*. As it
happens, the delivery of the parabasis is not
the sole duty of the *raisonneur*, for he performs
other functions of the chorus, of which multiple
personality he may be supposed to be a con-
densation into a single person. He listens to
the talk of the hero and of the heroine, taking
the part of the *confident* of French tragedy
(itself a feeble substitute for the chorus of
Greek tragedy) ; he asks the proper questions
to evoke the fullest expression of the hero's
and the heroine's sentiments ; he is properly
sympathetic ; and he also serves as a speaking-
trumpet for the author, being sometimes, as
in " Les Idées de Madame Aubrey," charged
with the utterance of the final moral.

To the ancient chorus and to the modern
raisonneur, there was even a mediæval analogue
In the interludes—which followed the mysteries

and the moralities, and which with them prepared players and playgoers for the coming
of the dramatized chronicle and of the romantic drama—"not infrequently," so Symonds
records in his " Shakespeare's Predecessors in
the English Drama " (p. 176) " a Doctor, sur-
viving from the Expositor of the miracles,
interpreted the allegory as the action pro-
ceeded."

1895.

THE WHOLE DUTY OF CRITICS.

"DOUBTLESS criticism was originally benignant, pointing out the beauties of a work rather than its defects. The passions of man have made it malignant, as the bad heart of Procrustes turned the bed, the symbol of repose, into an instrument of torture." So wrote Longfellow a many years ago, thinking, it may be, on "English bards and Scotch Reviewers," or on the Jedburgh justice of Jeffrey. But we may question whether the poet did not unduly idealize the past, as is the custom of poets, and whether he did not unfairly asperse the present. With the general softening of manners, no doubt those of the critic have improved also. Surely, since a time whereof the memory of man runneth not to the contrary, "to criticise," in the ears of many, if not of most, has been synonymous with "to find fault." In Farquhar's "Inconstant," now nearly two hundred years old, Petit says of a certain lady: "She's a critic, sir; she hates a jest, for fear it should please her."

The critics themselves are to blame for this misapprehension of their attitude.   When Mr. Arthur Pendennis wrote reviews for the " Pall Mall Gazette," he settled the poet's claims as though he " were my lord on the bench and the author a miserable little suitor trembling before him."   The critic of this sort acts not only as judge and jury, first finding the author guilty and then putting on the black cap to sentence him to the gallows, but he often volunteers as executioner also, laying on a round dozen lashes with his own hand, and with a hearty good-will.   We are told, for example, that Captain Shandon knew the crack of Warrington's whip and the cut his thong left.   Bludyer went to work like a butcher and mangled his subject, but Warrington finished a man, laying " his cuts neat and regular, straight down the back, and drawing blood every time."

Whenever I recall this picture I understand the protest of one of the most acute and subtle of American critics, who told me that he did not much mind what was said about his articles so long as they were not called "trenchant." Perhaps trenchant is the adjective which best defines what true criticism is not.   True criticism, so Joubert tells us, is " *un exercice méthodique de discernement*." It is an effort to understand and to explain.   The true critic is no more an executioner than he is an

assassin ; he is rather a seer, sent forward to
spy out the land, and most useful when he
comes back bringing a good report and bearing
a full cluster of grapes.

"*La critique sans bonté trouble le gout et
empoisonne les saveurs,*" said Joubert again ;
unkindly criticism disturbs the taste and
poisons the savour. No one of the great
critics was unkindly. That Macaulay merci-
lessly flayed Montgomery is evidence, were
any needed, that Macaulay was not one of the
great critics. The tomahawk and the scalping-
knife are not the critical apparatus, and they
are not to be found in the armoury of Lessing
and of Sainte-Beuve, of Matthew Arnold and
of James Russell Lowell. It is only inci-
dentally that these devout students of letters
find fault. Though they may ban now and
again, they came to bless. They chose their
subjects, for the most part, because they loved
these, and were eager to praise them and to
make plain to the world the reasons for their
ardent affection. Whenever they might chance
to see incompetence and pretension pushing
to the front, they shrugged their shoulders
more often than not, and passed by on the
other side silently :—and so best. Very rarely
did they cross over to expose an impostor.

Lessing waged war upon theories of art,
but he kept up no fight with individual authors.
Sainte-Beuve sought to paint the portrait of

the man as he was, warts and all ; but he did not care for a sitter who was not worth the most loving art. Matthew Arnold was swift to find the joints in his opponent's armour ; but there is hardly one of his essays in criticism which had not its exciting cause in his admiration for its subject. Mr. Lowell has not always hidden his scorn of a sham, and sometimes he has scourged it with a single sharp phrase. Generally, however, even the humbugs get off scot-free, for the true critic knows that time will attend to these fellows, and there is rarely any need to lend a hand. It was Bentley who said that no man was ever written down save by himself.

The late Edouard Scherer once handled M. Emile Zola without gloves ; and M. Jules Lemaître has made M. Georges Ohnet the target of his flashing wit. But each of these attacks attained notoriety from its unexpectedness. And what has been gained in either case? Since Scherer fell foul of him, M. Zola has written his strongest novel, "Germinal" (one of the most powerful tales of this century), and his rankest story, "La Terre" (one of the most offensive fictions in all the history of literature). M. Lemaître's brilliant assault on M. Ohnet may well have excited pity for the wretched victim ; and, damaging as it was, I doubt if its effect is as fatal as the gentler and more humorous criticism of M. Anatole

France, in which the reader sees contempt
slowly gaining the mastery over the honest
critic's kindliness.

For all that he was a little prim in taste
and a little arid in manner, Scherer had the
gift of appreciation—the most precious possession of any critic. M. Lemaître, despite
his frank enjoyment of his own skill in fence,
has a faculty of hearty admiration. There
are thirteen studies in the first series of his
" Contemporains," and the dissection of the
unfortunate M. Ohnet is the only one in which
the critic does not handle his scalpel with
loving care. To run amuck through the
throng of one's fellow-craftsmen is not a sign
of sanity :—on the contrary. Depreciation is
cheaper than appreciation ; and criticism
which is merely destructive is essentially inferior to criticism which is constructive. That
he saw so little to praise is greatly against
Poe's claim to be taken seriously as a critic ;
so is his violence of speech ; and so also is
the fact that those whom he lauded might be
as little deserving of his eulogy as those whom
he assailed were worthy of his condemnation.
The habit of intemperate attack which grew
on Poe is foreign to the serene calm of the
higher criticism. F. D. Maurice made the
shrewd remark that the critics who take
pleasure in cutting up mean books soon dete-
riorate themselves—subdued to that they work

in. It may be needful, once in a way, to nail
vermin to the barn door as a warning, and
thus we may seek a reason for Macaulay's
cruel treatment of Montgomery, and M.
Lemaître's pitiless castigation of M. Ohnet.
But in nine cases out of ten, or rather in
ninety-nine out of a hundred, the attitude of
the critic towards contemporary trash had
best be one of absolute indifference, sure that
Time will sift out what is good, and that Time
winnows with unerring taste.

The duty of the critic, therefore, is to help
the reader to "get the best"—in the old phrase
of the dictionary venders—to choose it, to
understand it, to enjoy it.   To choose it, first
of all ; so must the critic dwell with delighted
insistence upon the best books, drawing attention afresh to the old and discovering the new
with alert vision. Neglect is the proper portion
of the worthless books of the hour, whatever
may be their vogue for the week or the month.
It cannot be declared too frequently that
temporary popularity is no sure test of real
merit ; else were "Proverbial Philosophy," the
"Light of Asia," and the "Epic of Hades"
the foremost British poems since the decline
of Robert Montgomery ; else were the "Lamplighter" (does anyone read the "Lamplighter"
nowadays, I wonder ?), "Looking Backward,"
and "Mr. Barnes of New York" the typical
American novels.   No one can insist too often

on the distinction between what is "good
enough" for current consumption by a careless
public and what is really good, permanent,
and secure. No one can declare with too
much emphasis the difference between what
is literature and what is not literature, nor the
width of the gulf which separates them. A
critic who has not an eye single to this distinction fails of his duty. Perhaps the best
way to make the distinction plain to the reader
is to persist in discussing what is vital and
enduring, pointedly passing over what may
happen to be accidentally popular.

Yet the critic mischooses who should shut
himself up with the classics of all languages
and in rapt contemplation of their beauties be
blind to the best work of his own time. If
criticism itself is to be seen of men, it must
enter the arena and bear a hand in the combat. The books which have come down to us
from our fathers and from our grandfathers
are a blessed heritage, no doubt ; but there
are a few books of like value to be picked out
of those which we of to-day shall pass along
to our children and to our grandchildren. It
may be even that some of our children are
beginning already to set down in black and
white their impressions of life, with a skill and
with a truth which shall in due season make
them classics also. Sainte-Beuve asserted that
the real triumph of the critic was when the

poets whose praises he had sounded and for
whom he had fought grew in stature and surpassed themselves, keeping, and more than
keeping, the magnificent promises which the
critic, as their sponsor in baptism, had made
for them. Besides the criticism of the classics,
grave, learned, definitive, there is another more
alert, said Sainte-Beuve, more in touch with
the spirit of the hour, more lightly equipped,
it may be, and yet more willing to find
answers for the questions of the day. This
more vivacious criticism chooses its heroes
and encompasses them about with its affection, using boldly the words " genius " and
"glory," however much this may scandalize
the lookers-on :

" Nous tiendrons, pour lutter dans l'arène lyrique,
Toi la lance, moi les coursiers."

To few critics is it given to prophesy the
lyric supremacy of a Victor Hugo :—it was in
a review of " Les Feuilles d'Automne " that
Sainte-Beuve made this declaration of principles. A critic lacking the insight and the
equipment of Sainte-Beuve may unduly despise an Ugly Duckling, or he may mistake a
Goose for a Swan, only to wait in vain for its
song. Indeed, to set out of malice prepense
to discover a genius is but a wild-goose chase
at best ; and though the sport is pleasant for
those who follow, it may be fatal to the chance

fowl who is expected to lay a golden egg.
Longfellow's assertion that "critics are sen-
tinels in the grand army of letters, stationed
at the corners of newspapers and reviews to
challenge every new author," may not be altogether acceptable, but it is at least the duty of
the soldier to make sure of the papers of those
who seek to enlist in the garrison.

"British criticism has always been more or
less parochial," said Lowell, many years ago,
before he had been American Minister at St.
James's. "It cannot quite persuade itself that
truth is of immortal essence, totally independent of all assistance from quarterly journals
or the British army and navy." No doubt
there has been a decided improvement in the
temper of British criticism since this was
written ; it is less parochial than it was, and
it is perhaps now one of its faults that it
affects a cosmopolitanism to which it does not
attain. But even now an American of literary
taste is simply staggered—there is no other
word for it—whenever he reads the weekly
reviews of contemporary fiction in the " Athe-
næum," the " Academy," the " Spectator," and
the " Saturday Review," and when he sees high
praise bestowed on novels so poor that no
American pirate imperils his salvation to reprint them. The encomiums bestowed, for
example, upon such tales as those which are
written by the ladies who call themselves

" Rita," and " The Duchess " and " The
Authoress of 'The House on the Marsh,' "
seem hopelessly uncritical. The writers of
most of these reviews are sadly lacking in
literary perception and in literary perspective.
The readers of these reviews—if they had no
other sources of information—would never
suspect that the novel of England is no
longer what it was once, and that it is now
inferior in art to the novel of France and of
Spain, of Russia and of America. If the petty
minnows are magnified thus, what lens will
serve fitly to reproduce the lordly salmon or
the stalwart tarpon? Those who praise the
second-rate or the tenth-rate in terms appropriate only to the first-rate are derelict to the
first duty of the critic—which is to help the
reader to choose the best.

And the second duty of the critic is like
unto the first. It is to help the reader to
understand the best. There is many a book
which needs to be made plain to him who
runs as he reads, and it is the running reader
of these hurried years that the critic must
needs address. There are not a few works of
high merit (although none, perhaps, of the
very highest) which gain by being explained,
even as Philip expounded Esaias to the
eunuch of Candace, Queen of the Ethiopians,
getting up into his chariot and guiding him.
Perhaps it is paradoxical to suggest that a

book of the very highest class is perforce clear
beyond all need of commentary or exposition;
but it is indisputable that familiarity may blur
the outline and use may wear away the sharp
edges, until we no longer see the masterpiece
as distinctly as we might, nor do we regard it
with the same interest. Here again the critic
finds his opportunity ; he may show the
perennial freshness of that which seemed for
a while withered ; and he may interpret again
the meaning of the message an old book may
bring to a new generation. Sometimes this
message is valuable and yet invisible from the
outside, like the political pamphlets which
were smuggled into the France of the Second
Empire concealed in the hollow plaster busts
of Napoleon III., but ready to the hand that
knew how to extract them adroitly at the
proper time.

The third duty of the critic, after aiding the
reader to choose the best and to understand
it, is to help him to enjoy it. This is possible
only when the critic's own enjoyment is acute
enough to be contagious. However well informed a critic may be, and however keen he
may be, if he be not capable of the cordial admiration which warms the heart, his criticism
is wanting. A critic whose enthusiasm is not
catching lacks the power of disseminating his
opinions. His judgment may be excellent,
but his influence remains negative. One torch

may light many a fire ; and how far a little
candle throws its beams ! Perhaps the ability
to take an intense delight in another man's
work, and the willingness to express this delight frankly and fully, are two of the characteristics of the true critic ; of a certainty they
are the characteristics most frequently absent
in the criticaster. Consider how Sainte-Beuve
and Matthew Arnold and Lowell have sung
the praises of those whose poems delighted
them. Note how Mr. Henry James and M.
Jules Lemaître are affected by the talents of
M. Alphonse Daudet and of Guy de Maupassant.

Having done his duty to the reader, the
critic has done his full duty to the author also.
It is to the people at large that the critic is
under obligations, not to any individual. As
he cannot take cognizance of a work of art,
literary or dramatic, plastic or pictorial, until
after it is wholly complete, his opinion can be
of little benefit to the author. A work of art
is finally finished when it comes before the
public, and the instances are very few indeed
when an author has ever thought it worth
while to modify the form in which it was first
presented to the world. A work of science,
on the other hand, depending partly on the
exactness of the facts which it sets forth and
on which it is founded, may gain from the
suggested emendations of a critic. Many a

history, many a law book, many a scientific
treatise has been bettered in successive editions
by hints gleaned here and there from the reviews of experts.

But the work of art stands on a wholly
different footing from the work of science ;
and the critics have no further duty towards
the author, except, of course, to treat him
fairly, and to present him to the public if they
deem him worthy of this honour. The novel
or the poem being done once for all, it is
hardly possible for critics to be of any use to
the novelist or to the poet personally. The
artist of experience makes up his mind to this,
and accepts criticism as something which has
little or nothing to do with his work, but which
may materially affect his position before the
public. Thackeray, who understood the feelings and the failings of the literary man as no
one else, has shown us Mr. Arthur Pendennis
reading the newspaper notices of his novel,
"Walter Lorraine," and sending them home
to his mother. " Their censure did not much
affect him ; for the good-natured young man
was disposed to accept with considerable
humility the dispraise of others. Nor did
their praise elate him overmuch ; for, like
most honest persons, he had his own opinion
about his own performance, and when a critic
praised him in the wrong place he was hurt
rather than pleased by the compliment."

Mr. James tells us that the author of " Smoke "
and " Fathers and Sons," a far greater novelist
than the author of " Walter Lorraine," had a
serene indifference towards criticism. Turgenef
gave Mr. James " the impression of thinking
of criticism as most serious workers think of
it—that it is the amusement, the exercise, the
subsistence of the critic (and, so far as this goes,
of immense use), but that, though it may often
concern other readers, it does not much concern
the artist himself." Though criticism is of little
use to the author directly, it can be of immense
service to him indirectly, if it be exposition
rather than comment ; not a bald and barren
attempt at classification, but a sympathetic interpretation. At bottom, sympathy is the prime
requisite of the critic ; and with sympathy
come appreciation, penetration, revelation—
such, for example, as the American novelist
has shown in his criticisms of the Russian.

There is one kind of review of no benefit
either to the author or to the public. This is
the careless, perfunctory book-notice, penned
hastily by a tired writer, who does not take the
trouble to formulate his opinion, and perhaps
not even to form one. Towards the end of 1889
there appeared in a British weekly the following
notice of a volume of American short stories :

" A littery gent in one of Mr. [——]'s short
stories says : ' A good idea for a short story is a shy
bird, and doesn't come for the calling.' Alas !

alas ! it is true.   The French can call a great deal
better than we can ; but the Americans, it would
seem, cannot.   The best of Mr. [——]'s stories is
the first, about a tree which grew out of the bosom
of a buried suicide, and behaved accordingly to his
descendants ; but, so far from being a short story,
it is a long one, extending over some hundreds of
years, and it suffers from the compression which
Mr. [——] puts upon it.   It deserves to have a
volume to itself."

Refraining from all remark upon the style
in which this paragraph is written or upon the
taste of the writer, I desire to call attention to
the fact that it is not what it purports to be.
It is not a criticism within the accepted meaning of the word.   It indicates no intellectual
effort on the part of its writer to understand
the author of the book.   An author would
need to be superlatively sensitive who could
take offence at this paragraph, and an author
who could find pleasure in it would have to be
unspeakably vain.   To me this notice seems
the absolute negation of criticism—mere words
with no suggestion of a thought behind them.
The man who dashed this off robbed the
author of a criticism to which he was entitled
if the book was worth reviewing at all ; and in
thus shirking his bounden duty he also cheated
the proprietor of the paper who paid him.
Empty paragraphing of this offensive character
is commoner now than it was a few years ago,

commoner in Great Britain than in the United States, and commoner in anonymous articles than in those warranted by the signature of the writer.   Probably the man who was guilty of this innocuous notice would have been ashamed to put his name to it.

If a book is so empty that there is nothing to say about it, then there is no need to say anything.   It is related that when a dramatist, who was reading a play before the Committee of the Comédie Française, rebuked M. Samson for slumbering peacefully during this ceremony, the eminent comedian answered promptly, "Sleep, Monsieur, is also an opinion."   If a book puts the critic to sleep, or so benumbs his faculties that he finds himself speechless, he has no call to proceed further in the matter.   Perhaps the author may take heart of grace when he remembers that of all Shakespeare's characters it was the one with the ass's head who had an exposition of sleep come upon him, as it was the one with the blackest heart who said he was nothing if not critical.

If I were to attempt to draw up Twelve Good Rules for Reviewers, I should begin with:

I. Form an honest opinion.

II. Express it honestly.

III. Don't review a book which you cannot take seriously.

IV. Don't review a book with which you are out of sympathy.   That is to say, put yourself in the author's place, and try to see his work from his point of view, which is sure to be a coign of vantage.

V. Stick to the text. Review the book before you, and not the book some other author might have written ; *obiter dicta* are as value-less from the critic as from the judge. Don't go off on a tangent. And also don't go round in a circle. Say what you have to say, and stop. Don't go on writing about and about the subject, and merely weaving garlands of flowers of rhetoric.

VI. Beware of the Sham Sample, as Charles Reade called it. Make sure that the specimen bricks you select for quotation do not give a false impression of the *façade*, and not only of the elevation merely, but of the perspective also, and of the ground-plan.

VII. In reviewing a biography or a history, criticise the book before you, and don't write a parallel essay, for which the volume you have in hand serves only as a peg.

VIII. In reviewing a work of fiction, don't give away the plot. In the eyes of the novelist this is the unpardonable sin. And, as it dis-counts the pleasure of the reader also, it is almost equally unkind to him.

IX. Don't try to prove every successful author a plagiarist. It may be that many a successful author has been a plagiarist, but no author ever succeeded because of his plagiary.

X. Don't break a butterfly on a wheel.   If a book is not worth much, it is not worth reviewing.

XI. Don't review a book as an east wind would review an apple-tree—so it was once said Douglas Jerrold was wont to do. Of what profit to any one is mere bitterness and vexation of spirit?

XII. Remember that the critic's duty is to the reader mainly, and that it is to guide him not only to what is good, but to what is best. Three parts of what is contemporary must be temporary only.

Having in the past now and again fallen from grace myself and written criticism, I know that on such occasions these Twelve Good Rules would have been exceedingly helpful to me had I then possessed them ; therefore I offer them now hopefully to my fellow-critics. But I find myself in a state of humility (to which few critics are accustomed), and I doubt how far my good advice will be heeded. I remember that, after reporting the speech in which Poor Richard's maxims were all massed together, Franklin tells us that " thus the old gentleman ended his harangue. The people heard it and approved the doctrine ; and immediately practised the contrary, just as if it had been a common sermon."

1890.

H

TWO FRENCH DRAMATIC CRITICS.

I. M. FRANCISQUE SARCEY.

TO attempt a portrait of a man of letters after the subject has already sat to two limners as accomplished as Mr. Henry James and M. Jules Lemaître is venturesome and savours of conceit; but nearly fifteen years have passed since Mr. James made his off-hand thumbnail sketch of M. Sarcey; and M. Lemaître's more recent and more elaborate portraiture in pastels was intended to be seen of Parisians only. Moreover, Mr. James, although he praises M. Sarcey, does so with many reserves, not to say a little grudgingly; he even echoes the opinion once current in Paris that M. Sarcey is heavy—an opinion which M. Lemaître denounces and disproves.

It is in person that M. Sarcey is heavy—in body, not in mind. He is portly and thick-set, but not thick-witted. He is short-sighted physically, but no critic has keener insight. His judgments are as solid and as firm-footed as his tread. Sainte-Beuve has indicated the difference between the "grave, learned, de-

finitive" criticism which penetrates and explains and "the more alert, and more lightly
armed" criticism which gives the note to contemporary thought.   It is in the former class,
among the "grave, learned, definitive" critics
that M. Sarcey must be placed ; but his
serious and elaborate decisions are expressed
with perhaps as much liveliness and as much
point as any one of the "more alert and more
lightly armed" may display.   M. Sarcey's wit
is Voltairean in its quality, in its directness,
and in its ease.   Though his arm is strong to
smite a cutting blow if need be, yet more often
than not it is with the tip of the blade that
he punctures his adversary, fighting fairly and
breaking through the guard by skill of fence.

And of fighting M. Sarcey has had his fill
since he entered journalism more than thirty
years ago.   Born in 1828, he was admitted to
the Normal School in 1848 in the class with
Taine and Edmond About.   For seven years
after his graduation in 1851, he served as a
professor in several small towns, constantly
involved in difficulties with the officials of the
Second Empire.   In 1858 he gave up the
desk of the teacher for that of the journalist,
and coming up to Paris by the aid and advice
of About, he began to write for the "Figaro."
The next year the "Opinion Nationale" was
started, and M. Sarcey became its dramatic
critic.   In 1867 he transferred his services to

the " Temps," which is indisputably the ablest
and most dignified of all Parisian newspapers ;
and to the " Temps," in the number which
bears the date of Monday and which appears
on Sunday afternoon, M. Sarcey has been
contributing for now a quarter of a century
a weekly review of the theatres, slowly gaining
in authority until for a score of years at least
his primacy in Paris as a dramatic critic has
been beyond question.

In addition to this hebdomadal essay M.
Sarcey has descended daily into the thick of
contemporary polemics.   He writes an article
nearly every day on the topic of the hour.
When About started the " XIXe Siècle " after
the Prussian war, M. Sarcey was his chief
editorial contributor, leading a lively campaign against administrative abuses of all
kinds and exposing sharply the blunders of
the ecclesiastical propaganda.   He has little
taste for party politics, which seem to him
arid and fruitless ; but in the righting of
wrongs he is indefatigable, and in the discussion of urban improvements, entering with
ardour into all questions of water supply,
sewerage and the like.   And to the consideration of all these problems he brings the broad
common sense, the stalwart logic, the robust
energy which are his chief characteristics.   He
has common sense in a most uncommon degree ; and its exercise might be monotonous

if it were not enlivened by ironic and playful wit.

Calling on him one day a few summers ago and being hospitably received in the spacious library which his friend M. Charles Garnier, the architect of the Opéra, has arranged for him in the wide-windowed studio of a house purchased by him from the painter who had built it for his own use, M. Sarcey told me that he was a little surprised to discover that such reputation as he might have outside of his own country was chiefly as a dramatic critic, whereas in France he was known rather as a working journalist. Sitting on the broad, square lounge below the wide window—the famous *Divan Rouge* of which M. Sarcey himself has told the legend in the pages of a French review—I suggested that perhaps this was owing to the merely local interest of the subjects the daily journalist was forced to deal with, while the Parisian dramatic critic discussed plays, many of which were likely to be exported far beyond the boundaries of France and beyond the limits of the French language. I asked him also how it was that he had never made any collection of his dramatic criticisms, or even a selection from them, as Jules Janin and Théophile Gautier had done in the past, and as Auguste Vitu of the "Figaro" and M. Jules Lemaître of the "Débats" had more recently attempted.

I regret that I cannot recall the exact words of M. Sarcey's answer, although my recollection of the purport of his remarks is distinct enough. He said that he had not collected his weekly articles or even made a selection from them because they were journalism and not literature : the essential difference between journalism and literature being that the newspaper is meant for the moment only while the book is intended for all time, or as much of it as may be ; he wrote for the " Temps " his exact opinion at the minute of the writing and having in view all the circumstances of the hour. He said that in a book an author might be moderate in assertion, but that in a newspaper, which would be thrown away between sunrise and sunset, a writer at times must needs force the note ; and when it was worth while, he must be ready to declare his opinion loudly, with insistence and with undue emphasis. Of this privilege he had availed himself in the " Temps," and this was one reason why he did not wish to see his newspaper articles revived after they had done their work. (Here I feel it proper to note that a careful reading of M. Sarcey's feuilletons every week for now nearly twenty years has shown me that although his enthusiasm may seem at times a little overstrained, it is never factitious and it is never for an unworthy object.)

A second reason M. Sarcey gave for letting his dramatic criticisms sink into the oblivion of the back number is that he always gave his opinion frankly and fully at the instant when his impressions crystallized, and that he sometimes changed these opinions when a play was revived or when a player was seen in a new part. " Now, if I reprinted my feuilletons," said he, laughing, " I should lose the right to contradict myself."

" To look at all sides," Lowell tells us, " and to distrust the verdict of a single mood, is, no doubt, the duty of a critic," but the hasty review of a play penned before sunrise, while the printer's boy waits for copy, is of necessity the verdict of a single mood ; and this is why M. Sarcey feels the need of keeping his mind open to fresh impressions, and of holding himself in readiness to modify his opinion if good cause is shown for a reversal of the previous decision. And the criticism to which Lowell refers is, in one sense, literature, while the rapid reviewing of contemporary art can never be more than journalism, tinctured always with the belief that what is essential is news—first its collection, and secondarily a comment upon it.

In this same conversation with M. Sarcey in his library he told me that he had planned a book on the drama—" A History of Theatrical Conventions " was to be its exact title, I think

—but that he had done little or nothing towards it. The drama, like every other art, is
based upon the passing of an implied agreement between the public and the artist by
which the former allows the latter certain
privileges ; and in no art are these conventions more necessary and more obvious than
in the art of the stage. The dramatist has
but a few minutes in which to show his action,
and he can take the spectator to but a few
places ; therefore he has to select, to condense, to intensify beyond all nature ; and the
spectator has to make allowances for the needful absence of the fourth wall of the room in
which the scene passes, for the directness of
speech, for the omission of the non-essentials
which in real life cumber man's every movement. Certain of these conventions are permanent, immutable, inevitable, being of the
essence of the contract, as we lawyers say,
inherent in any conceivable form of dramatic
art. Certain others are accidental, temporary,
different in various countries and in various
ages.

A history of theatrical conventions as M.
Sarcey might tell it would be the story of
dramatic evolution and of the modification
of the art of the stage in accord with the
changing environment ; it would be as vital
and as pregnant and as stimulating a treatise
on the drama and its essential principles as

one could wish. I expressed to M. Sarcey
my eagerness to hold such a book in my
hand as soon as might be. He laughed again
heartily, and returned that he had made little
progress, and that he was in no hurry to set
forth his ideas nakedly by themselves and
systematically co-ordinated. "If I once formulated my theories," he said, "with what
could I fill my feuilleton—those twelve broad
columns of the 'Temps' every week?"

What M. Sarcy has not yet done for himself
the late Becq de Fouquières attempted in a
book on "L'Art de la Mise en Scène," the
principles laid down in which are derived
mainly from M. Sarcey's essays in the
"Temps." M. de Fouquières, it is to be noted,
had not M. Sarcey's knowledge, his authority,
his vigour, or his style, but his treatise is
logical and valuable, and may be recommended heartily to all students of the stage.

That M. Sarcey should ever feel any difficulty in filling his allotted space is incon-
ceivable to those who wonder weekly at his
abundance, his variety, and his overflowing
information. The post of dramatic critic has
been held in Paris by many distinguished
men, who for the most part regarded it with
distaste and merely as a disagreeable livelihood.
Théophile Gautier was frequent in his denunciation of his theatrical servitude, speaking of
himself as one toiling in the galley of jour-

nalism and chained to the oar of the feuilleton. In like manner Théodore de Banville and M. François Coppée cried aloud at their slavery, and sought every occasion for an excursus from the prescribed theatrical theme. Even M. Jules Lemaître now and again strays from the path to discuss in the " Débats " a novel or a poem not strictly within the jurisdiction of the dramatic critic. M. Sarcey is never faint in his allegiance to the stage, and he is never short of material for examination. If there are no novelties at the theatres, there may be new books about the stage. Or if these fail there are questions of theatrical administration. Or, in default of everything else, the Comédie-Française is always open, and in the dull days of the summer it acts the older plays, the comedies and tragedies of the classical repertory, and in these M. Sarcey finds many a peg on which to hang a disquisition on dramatic esthetics. I will not say that I have not found the same truth presented more than once in the eight or nine hundred of M. Sarcey's weekly essays that I have read and preserved, or the same moral enforced more than once ; but that is a pretty poor truth which will not bear more than one repetition.

Perhaps the first remark a regular reader of M. Sarcey's weekly review finds himself making is that the critic has a profound know-

ledge of the art of the stage. Of a certainty
the second is to the effect that the critic very
evidently delights in his work, is obviously
glad to go to the theatre and pleased to express his opinion on the play and the performance. No dramatic critic was ever more
conscientious than M. Sarcey, none was ever
as indefatigable. Often he returns to see a
piece a second time before recording his
opinion in print, ready to modify his first impression and quick to note the effect produced
on the real public, the broad body of average
playgoers who are but sparsely represented
on first nights.

Next to his enjoyment of his work and his
conscience in the discharge of his duty, the
chief characteristic of M. Sarcey is his extraordinary knowledge, his wide acquaintance
with the history of the theatre in Greece, in
Rome, and in France, his close hold on the
thread of dramatic development, and his firm
grasp of the vital principles of theatric art.
He understands as no one else the theory of
the drama, the why and the wherefore of
every cog-wheel of dramatic mechanism. He
seizes the beauty of technical details, and he
is fond of making this plain to the ordinary
playgoer, who is conscious solely of the result
and careless of the means. He has a marvellous faculty of seizing the central situation of
a play and of setting this forth boldly, dwelling

on the subsidiary developments of the plot
only in so far as they are needful for the
proper exposition of the more important
point.   By directing all the light on this
dominating and culminating situation, the one
essential and pregnant part of the piece, M.
Sarcey manages to convey to the reader some
notion of the effect of the acted play upon the
audience—a task far above the calibre of the
ordinary theatrical critics, who content themselves generally with a hap-hazard and hasty
summary of the plot, bald and barren.   From
M. Sarcey's criticism of a play in Paris it is
possible for an intelligent reader in London
or in New York to appreciate the effect of the
performance and to understand the causes of
its success or its failure.

His criticism—even when one is most in
disagreement with his opinions—is always
informed with an exact appreciation of the
possibilities and the limitations of the acted
drama.   Here is M. Sarcey's real originality
as a theatrical critic—that he criticises the
acted drama as something to be acted.   With
the possible exception of Lessing—whom he
once praised to me most cordially, declaring
that he was delighted whenever he took down
the " Dramaturgie " and chanced upon some
dictum of the great German critic confirmatory
of one of his own theories—with the exception of Lessing and of G. H. Lewes, M. Sarcey

is the first dramatic critic of literary equipment who did not consider a tragedy or a
comedy merely as literature and apart from
its effect when acted. La Harpe and Geoffroy
might have contented themselves with reading
at home the plays they criticised for all the
effect of the performance to be detected in
their comment. Janin and Gautier were little
better : to them a drama was a specimen of
literature, to be judged by the rules and
methods applicable to other specimens of
literature.

Now no view could be more unjust to the
dramatist. A play is written not to be read,
primarily, but to be acted ; and if it is a good
play it is seen to fullest advantage only when
it is acted. M. Coquelin has recently pointed
out that if Shakespeare and Molière, the
greatest two dramatists that ever lived, were
both careless as to the printing of their plays,
it was perhaps because both knew that these
plays were written for the theatre, and that
only in the theatre could they be judged properly. Seen by the light of the lamps a play
has quite another complexion from that it
bears in the library. Passages pale and dull,
it may be, when read coldly by the eye, are
lighted by the inner fire of passion when presented in the theatre ; and the solid structure
of action, without which a drama is naught,
may stand forth in bolder relief on the stage.

A play in the hand of the reader and a play
before the eye of the spectator are two very
different things ; and the difference between
them bids fair to grow apace with the increasing attention paid nowadays to the purely
pictorial side of dramatic art, to the costumes
and the scenery, to the illustrative business
and the ingenious management of the lights.
No one knows better than M. Sarcey how
sharp the difference is between the play on
the stage and the play in the closet, and no
one has indicated the distinction with more
acumen.   He judges the play before him as it
impresses him and the surrounding playgoers
at its performance in the theatre, and not as it
might strike him on perusal alone in his study.

And this is one reason why—if it were necessary to declare the order of the critical hierarchy
—I should rank M. Sarcey as a critic of the
acted drama more highly than any British
critic even of the great days of British dramatic
criticism, when Lamb and Hazlitt and Leigh
Hunt were practitioners of the art.   The task
of Hazlitt and of Leigh Hunt was far different
from M. Sarcey's.   The English drama of their
day was so feeble that few except professed
students of theatrical history can now recall
the names of any play or of any playwright of
that time ; and therefore the critics devoted
themselves almost altogether to an analysis of
the beauties of Shakespeare and of the art of

acting as revealed by John Philip Kemble, Sarah Siddons, and Edmund Kean. Lamb's subtle and paradoxical essays are retrospective, the best of them, and commemorate performers and performances held in affectionate remembrance. He wrote little about the actual present, and thus he avoided the double difficulty of dramatic criticism as M. Sarcey has to meet it to-day in France.

This double difficulty is, that when the dramatic critic has to review a new play he is called upon to do two things at once, each incompatible with the other : he has to judge the play, which he knows only through the medium of the acting, and he has to judge the acting, which he knows only as it is shown in the play ; and thus there is a double liability to error. Neither the dramatist nor the comedian stands before the critic simply and directly—each can be seen only as the other is able and' willing to declare him. It may be said that the dramatic critic does not see a new play—he sees only a performance, and this performance may be good or bad, may betray the author or reinforce him, may be fairly representative of his work and his wishes or may not. It is not the play itself that the critic sees—it is only the performance. If the play is in print, the critic may correct the impression of the single representation, or he may do so if the play be revived. Lamb

and Hazlitt and Leigh Hunt, dealing almost
wholly with the comedies and tragedies of the
past, all of which were in print and in their
possession for quiet perusal, had a far easier
task than M. Sarcey's ;—they had to do little
more than comment upon the acting or express
their pre-existing opinion of the play itself.
M. Sarcey has to judge both piece and the
acting at the same time, and he has to judge
the piece solely through the medium of the
acting, and the acting solely through the
medium of the piece ; and it may happen that
either medium refracts irregularly. Every
actor, every dramatic author, every theatrical
manager knows that there are " ungrateful
parts " and " parts that play themselves." Out
of the former the best actor can make but
little, and in the latter the defects of even the
poorest actor are disguised.

No dramatic critic is better aware of this
double difficuly than M. Sarcey, and no one is
more adroit in solving it.   As far as natural
gifts and an unprecedented experience can
avail, he avoids the danger.   He is open-
minded, slow to formulate his opinion and
always ready to give a play or a player a
rehearing.   He is never mean, never morose,
never malignant.   He is not one of the critics
who attack a living author with the callous
carelessness with which an anatomist goes to
work on a nameless cadaver.   He is no more

easy to please than any other expert whose
taste is fine, though his sympathies are broad ;
but when he is pleased he is emphatic in praise.
It was in the " Idle Man," in his wonderful
panegyric of Kean's acting, that Dana said,
" I hold it to be a low and wicked thing to
keep back from merit of any kind its due ; "
and M. Sarcey is of Dana's opinion. He is
capable of dithyrambic rhapsodies of eulogy
when he is trying to warm up the Parisian
public to a proper appreciation of M. Meilhac's
" Gotte " or " Décoré," for example ; and
although nobody can love New York more
than I do, sometimes one of the " Temps " reviews of a new play at the Vaudeville, of a
revival at the Odéon, or of a first appearance
at the Français is enough to make me homesick
for Paris.

As a critic even of the drama, M. Sarcey
has his limitations. He is now and then
insular—Paris (like New York) had its origin
on an island. At times he is dogmatic to the
verge of despotism. He has the defects of his
qualities ; and the first of his qualities is a
robust common sense, which is sometimes a
little commonplace and sometimes again a
little overwhelming, a little intolerant. Common sense is an old failing of the French.
" We have almost all of us," says M. Jules
Lemaître, " more or less Malherbe, Boileau,
Voltaire, and M. Thiers in our marrow." A

I

characteristic of all these typical Frenchmen
was pugnacity, and this is one of M. Sarcey's
most valuable qualities. He fights fair, but he
fights hard. His long campaign against M.
Duquesnel as the manager of the Odéon and
his repeated attacks on the theories of the late
M. Perrin, until the death of that administrator
of the Comédie-Française, are memorable
instances of M. Sarcey's tenacity. They are
instances also of his sagacity, for time has
proved the truth of his contentions. Again,
when M. Zola made a bitter and personal
retort to a plain-spoken criticism, M. Sarcey
returned an answer as good-tempered as anyone could wish, but as convincing and as cutting as any of M. Zola's many opponents could
desire. When M. Sarcey picks up the gauntlet,
he handles his adversary without gloves.

In the reply to M. Zola as elsewhere, M.
Sarcey confessed his abiding weakness—the
incurable habit of heterophemy which makes
him miscall names in almost every article he
writes, setting down " Edmond" when it should
be " Edward," and the like. But blunders of
this sort are but trifles which any alert proof-
reader might check, and which every careful
reader can correct for himself. They are all of a
piece with M. Sarcey's writing, which abounds
in familiarities, in slang, in the technical
terms of the stage, in happy-go-lucky allusions
often exceedingly felicitous, and in frequent

anecdotes from his wide reading or from his own experience. The result is a style of transparent ease and of indisputable sincerity. Nobody was ever in doubt as to his meaning at any time, or in doubt as to the reason why he meant what he said. To this sincerity M. Sarcey referred in his reply to M. Zola, and to it he owes, as he there declared, much of his authority as a dramatic critic. With the public, intelligence and knowledge count for much, and skill tells also, and so does wit ; but nothing is as important to a critic as a reputation for integrity, for frankness, for absolute honesty in the expression of his opinions.

To keep this reputation free from suspicion M. Sarcey declined to solicit the succession of Émile Augier in the French Academy. In a dignified and pathetic letter to the public, he declared that although he believed that most of the dramatists who belonged to the Forty Immortals would vote for him, and although he believed that both before his candidacy and after his election he could criticise the plays of these dramatists as freely as he did now, yet he did not believe that the public would credit him with this fortitude. " The authority of the critic lies in the confidence of the public," he wrote ; and if the public doubted whether he would speak the truth and the whole truth as frankly after he had been a candidate or after he had become an Acade-

mician, his opinion would lose half its weight.
To guard his freedom he told me once he had
refused all honours, even the cross of the
Legion of Honour. He declared in this letter
that he hesitated long, and that he knew the
sacrifice he was making. If journalism had
been without a representative in the Academy,
perhaps he might have felt it his duty to be a
candidate, but John Lemoinne was one of the
Forty, and there were already two or three
other journalists drawing nigh to the Academy,
" who will fill most brilliantly the place I give
up to them." He concluded by declaring that
his ambition was to have on his tombstone the
two words which would sum up his career—
" Professor and Journalist."

He began as a professor, as a teacher in the
schools, and now for thirty years he has been
a journalist, a teacher in the newspapers, loving
his work, and doing it with a conscience and a
fidelity which make it an honour to the modern
newspaper.

1890.

II. M. JULES LEMAÎTRE.

IN the evolution of literature three kinds of
critics have been developed. First in point
of time came the critic who spoke as one
having authority, who appealed to absolute
standards of taste, who had no doubt as to the
force of his criterions, who judged according
to the strict letter of the law, and who willingly
advised a poet to put his Pegasus out to grass
or ordered a writer of prose to send his stalk-
ing-horse to the knacker. This critic believed
in definite legislation for literature, and sometimes—when his name was Aristotle or Horace,
Boileau or Pope—he codified the scattered laws,
that all might obey them understandingly.
Macaulay was the last English critic of this
class, and even now many of his minor imi-
tators hand down their hebdomadal judgments
in the broad columns of British weeklies.   In
France there is to-day a man of force, acute-
ness, and individuality, M. Ferdinand Brunetière, who accepts this outworn creed of criticism, and who acts up to it conscientiously in
the " Revue des Deux Mondes."

The papal infallibility of the " Essay on

Criticism" began to be doubted toward the
end of the last century.   Lessing, for one, had
impulses of revolt against the rigidity of the
rules by which literature was limited ; but the
German protest of the Schlegels, for instance,
was rather against the restrictions of French
criticism than against a narrow method of
appreciating poetry.   Like the Irish clergy-
man who declared himself willing to "re-
nounce the errors of the Church of Rome and
to adopt those of the Church of England,"
most of the writers who refused to be judged
by the precepts of Classicism were ready to
apply with equal rigour the rules of Romanticism.   But in time, out of the welter and
struggle of faction came a perception of a new
truth—that it is the task of the critic not to
judge, but to examine, to inquire, to investi-
gate, to see the object as it really is and to
consider it with disinterested curiosity.   This
Sainte-Beuve attempted, though even he did
not always attain to the lofty ideal he proclaimed ; and to the same chilly height
Matthew Arnold tried to reach, saying that
he wished to decide nothing as of his "own
authority ; the great art of criticism is to get
one's self out of the way and to let humanity
decide."

The phrase which Dr. Waldstein quoted
from Spinoza not long ago as characteristic of
the scientific mind—*Neque flere, neque ridere,*

neque admirare, neque contemnere, sed intelli-
gere (Neither to weep nor to laugh, neither to
admire nor to despise, but to understand)—
this may serve to indicate the aim of scientific
criticism which judges not, which expresses no
opinions, which does not take sides, which
merely sets down, with the arid precision of
an affidavit, the facts as these are revealed by
a qualitative analysis. Unfortunately, criticism as impersonal as this is impossible ; no
man can make a mere machine of himself to
register *in vacuo.* " If there were any recognized standard in criticism, as in apothecaries'
measure, so that, by adding a grain of praise
to this scale or taking away a scruple of blame
from that, we could make the balance mani-
festly even in the eyes of all men, it might
be worth while to weigh Hannibal," Lowell
tells us ; " but when each of us stamps his
own weights and warrants the impartiality of
his own scales, perhaps the experiment may
be wisely foregone."

The natural reaction from an impossibly
callous scientific criticism which sought to
suppress the personality of the critic was a
criticism which was frankly individual. This
is the third kind of criticism ; it abdicates all
inherited authority and it does not pretend to
scientific exactitude. It recognizes that no
standard is final, and that there is no disputing about tastes. It is aware that in the

higher criticism as in the higher education
there has been an abolition of the marking
system, and that the critic is no longer a
pedant or a pedagogue sending one author up
to the head of his class and setting another in
the corner with a fool's cap on his brow. It
declares the honest impression of the individual at the moment of writing, not concealing
the fact that even this may be different at
another time. In reality Poe was a critic of
this type, though he lacked frankness, and
with characteristic charlatanry was prompt to
appeal to the immutable standards to verify
his own vagaries.

The three types of criticism have been
evolved inevitably one out of the other ; and
the development of the third kind has not
driven out the practitioners of the first and
second. Critics of all three classes exist at
present side by side in France, England, and
America, disputing together daily in the
schools. Yet the man is of more importance
than the method ; and a born critic can bend
any theory of his art to suit his purpose.
Boileau and Sainte-Beuve were both good
critics, and Matthew Arnold was a good
critic ; and so was Lowell, who seemed rather
an eclectic, not firm in following any one
creed. To which theory a man gives in allegiance nowadays is mainly a question of tem-
perament. In France, as it happens, the most

brilliant critic of the younger generation, M. Jules Lemaître, belongs to the third class. M. Lemaître is a triumphant exemplar of individual criticism, giving his opinions for what they are worth, and presenting them so forcibly, so picturesquely, so pleasantly, that at least they are always worth listening to. There is no pose in his frankness, and his apparent inconsequence is open and honest.

In some respects M. Jules Lemaître is a typical Frenchman of letters. He has the ease, the grace, the wit, the lightness of touch, and the certainty of execution characteristic of the best French authors. Behind these charms he has the love of clearness, of order, of symmetry—in a word, of art—which is among the most marked of French qualities. He dislikes extravagance of any kind; he hates harshness, violence, brutality. He inherits the Latin tradition, and he has fed fat on the poetry of Greece and Rome. He has none of the liking of his contemporary, M. Paul Bourget, for foreign countries, and none of M. Bourget's curiosity as to foreign literature. M. Lemaître is content to have M. Pierre Loti do his travelling for him, or to let Guy de Maupassant go abroad as his proxy.

M. Jules Lemaître has not yet "come to forty years." He is still a young man. He was born in 1853, in the little village of Vennecy, on the edge of the forest of Orléans. He

attended school at Orléans and then in Paris,
and when he was nineteen he entered the
Normal School, which of late years has given
many a brilliant man to French literature. In
1875, at the age of twenty-two, he was gradu-
ated from the Normal School with high
honours, and he was at once sent to the
Lycée of Havre as professor of rhetoric. Here
he stayed five years teaching, and yet finding
time to write that first volume of verse with
which most authors begin their literary career.

In 1880 he published these poems, and in
the same year he was promoted and sent to
Algiers. In 1883 he brought out a second
book of rhymes, and he presented his double
theses to the Sorbonne, whereupon he was
made a doctor of letters. The thesis in French,
a study of the plays of Dancourt and of the
course of French comedy after the death of
Molière, was quite unconventional in its indi-
dividuality, as any one may see now that it
has been published. He was again promoted,
but he already thought of giving up his pro-
fessorship to venture into literature. In 1884
he asked for leave of absence and went to
Paris, where he began to contribute regularly
to the "Revue Bleue," the most literary and
the most independent of French weekly journals—as far as may be the Parisian equivalent
of the "Nation." In a very few weeks he
made his name known to all the Parisians

who care for literature. His acute analysis of
Renan was the first of his essays to attract
general attention ; and when he followed this
up with equally incisive studies of M. Zola
and of M. Georges Ohnet, he was at once
accepted as one of the most acute of contemporary French critics. As one of his bio-
graphers declares, " He was unknown in Octo-
ber, 1884, and in December he was famous."
A few months later, when J. J. Weiss resigned,
M. Lemaître was appointed dramatic critic of
the " Journal des Débats," the position long
held by Jules Janin.

His contributions to the " Revue Bleue "
M. Lemaître has four times gathered into
volumes sent forth under the same title, " Les
Contemporains." Selections from his weekly
articles in the " Débats " have also been
collected in successive volumes called " Impressions de Théâtre." The titles he has given
to these two series of his criticisms reveal the
aim of M. Lemaitre and his range. Those
whom he criticises are chiefly his contemporaries, or at furthest those who have deeply
and immediately influenced the men of to-
day ; and the criticisms themselves are chiefly
his impressions. M. Lemaître is a man of the
nineteenth century, first of all, and he tells
his fellow-men how the books and the plays
of the nineteenth century, the authors and the
actors, affect him, how they move him—in

short, how they impress him at the moment
regardless of any change of opinion which
may come to him in the future.

Sainte-Beuve protests against those who
borrow ready-made opinions, and it must be
admitted that more often than not a ready-
made opinion is a misfit. M. Jules Lemaître
has his opinions made to measure, and as soon
as he outgrows them they are cast aside.
While he wears them they are his own, and
neither in cut, cloth, nor style are they
commonplace. He has the double qualifica-
tion of the true critic—insight and equipment.
He has humour and good-humour, and he en-
joys the play of his own wit. He is a scholar
who is often as lively and as lawless as a
schoolboy. He is at once a man of letters
and a man of the world. He hates the smell
of the lamp, and his best work has the flavour
of the good talk that may go up the chimney
when there is a wood fire on the hearth. As
he gained experience and authority he has
become less emphatic, and he hesitates more
before coming to definite conclusions. The
certainty of conviction which he brought with
him from the provinces has given way to a
more Parisian scepticism. His earlier criticisms
were all solidly constructed and stood four-
square. Renan, M. Georges Ohnet, and M. Zola
were never in any doubt as to his final opinion.
The later criticisms are more individual,

more "personal"—as the French say—more impressionist, than the earlier. M. Lemaître is quite aware that the shield is silver on one side and gold on the other, and he is no longer willing to break a lance for either metal, whichever may be nearer to him. He is open-minded, he sees both sides at once, and he sets down both the pro and the con., sometimes declining to express his own ultimate opinion, sometimes even refusing to form any opinion at all. He is fond of setting up a man of straw to act as the devil's advocate ; but though this insures a full hearing of the witnesses for the defence as well as for the prosecution, it rarely prevents M. Lemaître from getting his saint, after all, when he is resolute for the beatification. Now and again he seems indifferent, and he remains "on the fence," as we Yankees say, or rather on both sides of it at once. His attitude then is that of a lazy judge leaving the whole burden of decision on the jury. Yet he is prompt enough, as the essays on M. Daudet's "Immortel," on M. Zola's "Rêve," on Victor Hugo's "Toute la Lyre," in the fourth series, show plainly, when his opinion is clear and simple. This is evidence, were any needed, that behind the hesitation and the apparent indifference there is a live interest in literature, a real love for what is true, genuine, hearty, and a sharp hatred for shams.

His hatred of shams is shown in his swift condemnation of M. Georges Ohnet's romances, perhaps unduly ferocious in manner, although indisputably deserved. M. Georges Ohnet is the most popular of French novelists ; his stories sell by the hundred thousand, and he occupies the place in France which the late E. P. Roe held in America, and which Mr. Rider Haggard long held in England. There had been a general silence in the French press about M. Ohnet's novels ; no one praised them highly, but they pleased the public—or, at least, the half-educated and really illiterate mass of novel readers. M. Lemaître felt the revolt of a scholar of refined tastes and delicate instincts against the overpowering popularity of M. Ohnet's empty triviality, and in a memorable article he "belled the cat" and he "rang the bell." Never was such an execution since Macaulay slew Montgomery. M. Lemaître began by saying that he was in the habit of discussing literary subjects, but he hoped that he would be pardoned if he spoke now of the novels of M. Georges Ohnet ; and then he went on to hold up to scorn the feeble style of M. Ohnet, the merely mechanical structure of his stories, the conventionality of his characters and their falsity to humanity, the barren absurdity of his philosophy of life and the baseness of his appeal to the prejudices of the middle class, wherein he sought for readers. In general, M. Lemaître is keen of fence, and his weapon is the small sword of the duelling field ; but to M. Ohnet he took a single-stick or a quarter-staff, and with this he beat his victim black and blue, breaking more than one bone.

Longfellow tells us that " a young critic is like a boy with a gun ; he fires at every living thing he sees ; he thinks only of his own skill, not of the pain he is giving." M. Lemaître was a young critic when he wrote this crushing assault on M. Ohnet. Since then he has never attempted to repeat the experience ; it is true that there is in France to-day no other subject as good as M. Ohnet for a severe critic to try his hand on. Of late when M. Lemaître has had to express a hostile opinion he has been more indirect ; and now he draws blood by a dexterous insinuation adroitly thrust under his adversary's sword arm. Ill-disguised was his contempt for Albert Wolff, a Parisian from Cologne, a writer of *chroniques* for the " Figaro "—most perishable of all *articles de Paris*—one who was to journalism what M. Georges Ohnet is to literature. Ill-disguised is his condemnation of the part M. Henri Rochefort has played in the French politics of the past quarter of a century, and bitterly incisive—corrosive almost—is the outline he etches of the character of the man with the immitigable grin, the man whose

"Lanterne" helped to light the fall of the second empire, the man who has since egged on every revolt, however bloody, however hopeless, however foolish.

Of these adverse criticisms there are very few indeed—a scant half-dozen, perhaps—in the threescore essays contained in volumes of "Les Contemporains." This is as it should be, for he is a very narrow critic indeed who deals more in blame than in praise. For criticism to be profitable and pregnant, the critic must needs dwell on the works he admires. Merely negative criticism is sterile. The late Edmond Scherer said that "the ideal of criticism was to be able to praise cordially and with enthusiasm, if need be, without losing one's head or getting blind to defects."

Nothing is more needful for a critic than sympathy with his subject. The faculty of appreciation, of hearty admiration, of contagious enthusiasm even, is among the best gifts of a true critic; and this M. Lemaître has in abundance. He likes the best and the best only, but this he likes superlatively. And he can see the good points even of authors who do not altogether please him; and these he is always ready to laud in hearty fashion.

"Readers like to find themselves more severe than the critic; and I let them have this pleasure," said Sainte-Beuve. M. Lemaître goes far beyond his great predecessor;

he delights in broad eulogy of those who
appeal to his delicate sense of the exquisite
in literary art. His enjoyment of Pierre
Loti, for example, of M. Daudet's " Nabab,"
of Renan, is so intense that he is swept off his
feet by the strong current of admiration. But
though he lose his feet he keeps his head, and
in his highest raptures he is never uncritical.
What M. Lemaître likes best, if not always
the books best worth liking, are always at
least books well worth liking ; and he likes
them for what is best in them, and never for
their affectations, their superfluities, their contortions ; and it is for these often that many
a critic pretends to worship a master. M.
Lemaître's taste is keen and fine and sure ;
and his judgment is solid.

Although M. Lemaître knows his classics
—Greek, Latin, and French—as becomes a
Normalien, he likes French literature better
than Greek or Latin ; and he likes the French
literature of the nineteenth century better
than that of the eighteenth, or even of the
seventeenth. It is his contemporaries who
most interest him. In his clear and subtle
and respectful analysis of the characteristics
of his fellow-critic M. Ferdinand Brunetière,
M. Lemaître confesses that while he reads
Bossuet and acknowledges the power of that
most eloquent of orators, yet the reading gives
him little pleasure, " whereas often on opening

K

by chance a book of to-day or of yesterday"
he thrills with delight; and he calls on M.
Brunetière to set off one century against the
other. "If, perhaps, Corneille, Racine, Bossuet
have no equivalents to-day, the great century
had no equivalent of Lamartine, of Victor
Hugo, of Musset, of Michelet, of George Sand,
of Saint-Beuve, of Flaubert, of M. Renan.
And is it my fault if I would rather read a
chapter of M. Renan than a sermon of Bossuet,
the "Nabab" than the "Princess of Cleves,"
and a certain comedy of Meilhac and Halèvy
even than a comedy of Molière?"

It is this, I think, which gives to M. Lemaître's criticism much of its value—his intense liking for the French literature of to-day,
and his perfect understanding of its moods
and of its methods. He has an extraordinary
dexterity in plucking out the heart of technical
mysteries. In considering a little book of
sayings he took occasion to declare the theory
of maxim-making, whereby every man may
be his own La Rochefoucauld, and he sup-
plied an abundance of bright examples manufactured according to his new formulas. In
like manner he discovered the trick of the
rhythms and rhymes of Théodore de Banville,
the reviver of the rondeau and of the ballade,
and a past-master of verbal jugglery and of
acrobatic verse.

In peering into the methods of more im-

portant literary workmen he is equally acute
Take, for example, his study of M. Zola—
perhaps the most acute and the most respectful analysis of M. Zola's very remarkable
powers to be found anywhere ; more elaborate
than the excellent essay written by Mr. Henry
James when " Nana " was published. M. Zola
is a novelist with a theory of his art violently
promulgated and turbulently reiterated until
most people were ready to accept his own
word for his work, and to regard his romances
as examples of the Naturalism he proclaimed.
Now and then an adverse critic dwelt on the
inconsistencies between M. Zola's theory and
his practice, and M. Zola himself bemoaned
the occasional survivals of the Romanticist
spirit he detected in himself. M. Lemaître
began by thrusting this aside, and by painting
M. Zola in his true colours with a bold sweep
of the brush. " M. Zola," he declared, " is not
a critic, and he is not a Naturalistic novelist
in the meaning he himself gives to the term.
But M. Zola is an epic poet and a pessimistic
poet. . . . By poet I mean a writer who in
virtue of an idea . . . notably transforms
reality, and having so transformed it gives it
life." M. Lemaître then shows us the simple
but powerful mechanism of M. Zola's art—
how he takes a theme and sets it before the
reader with broad strokes and with typical
characters boldly differentiated and reduced

almost to their elements, but none the less
alive. Space fails here to show how M. Lemaître works out most convincingly the sub-
stantial identity of M. Zola's massive method
with that of the epic poet, and how he dis-
covers in every one of M. Zola's later fictions
a Beast, a huge symbol of the theme which
that story sets forth, and a Chorus which comments upon the events and brings them nearer
to the reader.

The essay may be recommended to all who
have a taste for criticism ; I know nothing at
once more acute, more original, or truer. It
may be recommended especially to those who
would like to know what manner of writer
M. Zola is, and who yet shrink from the
reading of his novels, often drawn out and
wearisome, and nearly always foul and re-
pulsive. It is M. Zola's misfortune—and it
is indubitably his own fault—that he is judged
by hearsay often, and that his books are taken
as the types of filthy fiction. Perhaps he is
more frequently condemned than read—
although sometimes the British abuse of his
books has struck me as the reaction of guilty
enjoyment. Occasion serves to say in paren-
theses here that while M. Zola's forcible and
effective novels are painful often, while they
are dirty frequently and indefensibly, they are
not immoral. It is rather in Octave Feuillet's
rose-coloured novels or in M. Georges Ohnet's

gilt-edged fictions that we may seek insidious immorality.

M. Lemaître indicates the misplaced dirt in M. Zola's novels, and obviously enough is himself a man of clean mind ; but perhaps he lacks the inherent sternness of morality which in a man of Anglo-Saxon stock would go with an upright character like his.   He has a respectful regard for the Don Juan of Molière and of Mozart, of Byron and of Musset ; and he has a kindly tolerance for the disciples of Don Juan who infest French literature.

M. Lemaître's dramatic criticisms, his " Impressions de Théâtre," are quite as original as his more solid literary portraits, quite as fresh, quite as individual, quite as amusing.   He lacks the profound knowledge of the conditions of dramatic art, the extraordinary insight into the necessary conventions upon which it is based, the thorough acquaintance with the history of the theatre in France, which have given to the foremost theatrical critic of our time, M. Francisque Sarcey, his unexampled authority.   But he looks at the stage always through his own eyes, never through the opera-glass of his neighbour or the spectacles of tradition.   He is fond of the theatre, and yet he readily goes outside of its walls and considers not merely the technic of the dramatist but also the ethics.   Like most well-equipped and keen-witted critics, his criticism willingly broadens its vision to consider life as well as literature. Of the conventionalities and the concessions to chance which the writer of comedy avails himself freely, M. Lemaître is tolerant, and wisely; but he is intolerant and implacable towards the false psychology and the defective ethics of the mere playwright who twists characters and misrepresents humanity to gain an effect.

The critic of the "Débats" is not content with describing the dramas of the leading theatres of Paris; he has a Thackerayan fondness for spectacles of all kinds, for the ballet, for the circus and the pantomime, for side-shows, for freaks of every degree. In all these he finds unfailing amusement and an unflagging variety of impressions. He is always alert, lively, gay; and though he travels far afield, he is never at his wits' end. In his dramatic criticisms M. Lemaître appears to me as a serious student of literature and of life, playing the part of a Parisian— and it is a most excellent impersonation.

Of M. Lemaître's poems, there is no need to say anything; they are the verses of a very clever man, no doubt, but not those of a born poet. They shine with the reflected light of his work in prose. Gray thought " even a bad verse as good a thing or better than the best observation that ever was made upon it " ; but even fairly good verse is not as good a thing as the best observation that ever was made on the best verse. It is the prose and not the verse of Lessing and of Saint-Beuve that we turn to, again and again.

Of M. Lemaître's stories there is no need to say much : they are the tales of a very clever man, of course, but not those of a born teller of tales. They lack a something vague and indefinable—a flavour, a perfume, an aroma of vitality ; it is as though they were a manufacture, rather, and not a growth. They are not inevitable enough. They are *naïf* without being quite convincing. They have simplicity of motive, harmony of construction, sharpness of outline, touches of melancholy and pathos, unfailing ingenuity and wit—and yet—and yet— Of the stories contained in the beautifully illustrated volume called "Dix Contes" only three or four are modern, and even these seem to have a hint of allegory as though there were perhaps a concealed moral somewhere. The rest are tales of once-upon-a-time, in Arabia, in Greece, in Rome, as dissimilar as possible from the *contes* of M. Daudet or of Maupassant, of M. Coppée or of M. Halévy, and with a certain likeness to the "Contes Philosophiques" of Voltaire. To say this is to suggest that they are rather fables, apologues, allegories, than short stories.

Of M. Lemaître's play, " Revoltée," there is

no need to say more ; it is the comedy of a
very clever man indeed, but not that of a born
playwright. When acted at the Odéon in
1889 it did not fail, but it did not prove a
powerful attraction. When published — and
to the delight of all who are fond of the drama
French plays are still published as English
comedies were once—it impressed the expert
as likely to read better than it acted. There
was abundance of wit, for example, but it was
rather the wit of M. Jules Lemaître than of
his characters, and it was rather the wit of the
study than of the stage. Yet "Revoltée" is
an honourable attempt, and highly interesting
to all who are interested in M. Lemaître.

To sum up my opinion of these tentative
endeavours in other departments of literature,
M. Lemaître is a very clever man, whose
cleverness does not lead him naturally and
irresistibly to poetry or to story-telling or to
playwriting. What it does lead him to is
criticism—criticism of literature primarily, because he loves letters, but criticism also of life
at large, of man and his manners, his motives,
his relation to the world and to the universe.
He has not only the faculty of straight thinking, but also that of plain speaking. He is
bold and direct in his discussion of social
problems, applying to their solution an unusual common sense, and developing also an
unusual understanding of the causes of ap-

parent anomalies.   I do not know anywhere a more acute statement of the relative duty of faithfulness on the part of husband and wife than is to be found in his criticism of the " Francillon " of M. Dumas *fils*.   And that this statement should be found in a theatrical criticism is characteristic of M. Lemaître's attitude; as his vision broadens and his interest in life deepens, a play or a novel is to him chiefly valuable as the theme and text of a social inquiry.   Literature alone no longer satisfies.

1890.

TWO SCOTSMEN OF LETTERS.

I. MR. ANDREW LANG.

THE most lifelike photograph of a friend is no more than a reminder of what we have seen for ourselves, since the camera has neither insight nor imagination ; a portrait by a true artist may bring out qualities but doubtfully glimpsed before, or it may even reveal depths of character hitherto unsuspected. In one of the London exhibitions during the season of 1885, amid many a "portrait of a gentleman," there was at least one portrait of a man—nervous, significant, vital. At a glance it was obvious that the man here depicted was a gentleman and a scholar, although the picture had none of the prim propriety of the ordinary academic portrait. There was an air of distinction about the sitter, twisted around in his chair, with his frankly humorous gaze. The casual stranger whose eye might fall on the painting could not but feel that the restless attitude was inevitably characteristic, and he could not but confess the charm of a most interesting personality. And, indeed, Mr.

Richmond's picture of Mr. Andrew Lang seems to me one of the most successful of modern portraits.

Perhaps the first effect it made on the beholder was to suggest the extreme cleverness of its subject—an effect which does but scant justice to Mr. Lang, for cleverness is best as an extra, as the superfluity of him who has some quality other and better. Molière was not clever, and M. Sardou is clever beyond belief. When cleverness is all a man's having, though he make a brave show for a while, he is poor indeed. Cleverness Mr. Lang has, and a plethora of it; but he has also a richer endowment. He may be called the Admirable Crichton of modern letters; and he is a graduate of St. Andrew's, that ancient Scottish university where the original Crichton was once a student, three centuries earlier. Thence he went to Oxford, where there lingered memories of Landor and Shelley, where he took the Newdigate prize for poetry, and where in due season he was elected a Fellow of Merton, the college of Anthony Wood. Herein, I think, we may grasp the clue to Mr. Lang's character, and to his career : he is a Scotsman who has been tinctured by Oxford, but who still grips his stony native land with many a clinging radicle.

Mr. Andrew Lang and Mr. Robert Louis Stevenson are the two Scottish chiefs of litera-

ture to-day. Both live out of Scotland, yet
both are loyal to the land of their birth, and
love it with all the ardour of a good son's love.
Neither is in robust health, but there is no
taint of invalidism in the writings of either, no
hint of morbid complaint or of unwholesome
self-compassion. Both are resolutely optimistic, as becomes Scotchmen. Both are critics,
with sharp eyes for valuing, and with a faculty
of enthusiastic and appetizing enjoyment of
what is best. They have both attempted
fiction, and both belong to the romantic school.
In differing degrees each is a poet, and each is
master of a prose than which no better is
written in our language nowadays. Mr. Lang's
style has not the tortured felicity of Mr. Stevenson's ; its happiness is easier and less wilful.
The author of " Letters to Dead Authors " is
not an artificer of cunning phrase like the
author of " Memories and Portraits ; " his style
is not hand-made nor the result of taking
thought ; it grows more of its own accord.
The style of each is transparent, but while Mr.
Stevenson's is as hard as crystal, Mr. Lang's is
fluid like water ; it flows, and sometimes it
sings as it flows, like the beautiful brooks he
longs to linger beside, changing with the sky
and the rocks and the trees, but always pure,
and limpid, and delightful.
    American readers, annoyed at the slovenli-
ness of most modern British essayists, are

struck by the transparent clearness of Mr.
Lang's style ; for though he was born north
of the Tweed his pages are spoilt by no Scot-
ticisms, and though he dwells by the banks of
the Thames they are disfigured by no Briti-
cisms. They are free from the doubtful English which has "the largest circulation in the
world." A constant perusal of the fine prose
of the great Frenchmen whom Mr. Lang
admires may have tended to keep his own
paragraphs free from blemish ; and a devoted
study of the great Greeks whom he loves may
have helped to give his pages their dignified
ease.

In his pellucid prose, as in his intellectual
alertness and in his lightness of touch, Mr.
Lang is rather French than English. He is a
nephew of Voltaire, and a cousin of M. Jules
Lemaître. As we read his graceful and nervous sentences sometimes our ear catches an
echo of Thackeray's cadences : and it was in
France that Thackeray served his apprentice-
ship to the trade of author. Sometimes our
eye rejoices in the play of a humour always
lambent and often Lamb-like ; and it is
perhaps from Charles Lamb that Mr. Lang
has got the knack of the quotation held in
solution. Like Dryden and Burke and
Bagehot, three masters of English prose, Mr.
Lang quotes abundantly and from a full
memory, and not always exactly. "Verify

your quotations " is not a warning that he has taken to heart. The books from which he can draw illustrations at will are numberless, and they are to be found in every department of the library. In Greek literature, and in French as well as in English, he has the minute thoroughness of the scholar ; but his main reading seems to have been afield, as happens to every man who loves books, and who likes to browse among them without let or hindrance.

The equipment of a critic Mr. Lang has, and the insight, and also the sympathy, without which the two other needful qualities lose half their value. There are limits to his sympathy, and he tells us that he does " not care for Mr. Gibbon except in his autobiography, nor for the elegant plays of M. Racine, nor very much for Mr. William Wordsworth, though his genius is undeniable " ; but the range of his knowledge and of his understanding seems to me wider than that of any other contemporary British critic. He is unfailing in affection for Homer, Herodotus, Theocritus, and Lucian, for Virgil and Horace, for Rabelais, Molière, and Dumas, for Shakespeare, Fielding, Miss Austen, and Thackeray, for Scott and Burns. He delights in the skittish writings of the lively lady who calls herself "Gyp," while for the psychologic subtleties of M. Paul Bourget he cares as little as does

" Gyp" herself. He was prompt in praise of
the author of " King Solomon's Mines ; " in
fact, Mr. Haggard's tales of battle, murder,
and suden death have found no warmer
eulogist than the author of " Ballades in Blue
China."

Longfellow declared that "many readers
judge of the power of a book by the shock it
gives their feelings, as some savage tribes de-
termine the power of muskets by their recoil ;
that being considered the best which fairly
prostrates the purchaser." Mr. Lang's taste
is too refined for this saying to be justly applicable to him ; but he does not think the worse
of a book because it tells a tale of daring-do.
He is eager for a story of

> ". . . battles, sieges, fortunes,
>
> . . . .
>
> Of moving accidents by flood and field,
> Of hair-breadth 'scapes i' the imminent deadly
>   breach."

He is quick to give a cordial greeting to a
traveller's history of " antres vast and deserts
idle," of " Anthropophagi, and men whose heads
do grow beneath their shoulders." In other
words, Mr. Lang is a romanticist to the bitter
end. Broad as his sympathy is, it is not
broad enough to comprehend realism. He is
restive when realism is lauded. Unconsciously,
no doubt, he resents it a little, and he does not
quite understand it. Mr. Lang can enjoy

Rabelais, and praise him for the qualities which make him great in spite of his wilful foulness ; but in M. Zola Mr. Lang sees little to commend. Quite the most perfunctory essay of Mr. Lang's that I ever read was one on the author of " L'Assommoir," which did but scant justice to the puissant labourer who toiled unceasingly on the massive edifice of the " Rougon-Macquart" series, as mightily planned and solid in structure as a mediæval cathedral, and, like it, disfigured and defiled by needless and frequent indecencies. Tolerant toward most literary developments, Mr. Lang is a little intolerant toward the analysts. Amiel delights him not, nor Marie Bashkirtseff either ; and it irks him to hear Ibsen praised, or Tolstoi, though the pitiful figure of Anna Karénina lingers in his memory. And as for Mr. Howells, it is hard to say whether it is as novelist or critic that he irritates Mr. Lang more. Mr. Howells once spoke of the critical essaylets which issued monthly from the " Editor's Study " as " arrows shot into the air in the hope that they will come down somewhere and hurt somebody." Enough of them have hit Mr. Lang to make him look like St. Sebastian, if only he had not plucked them out swiftly, one by one, and sent them hurtling back across the Atlantic. Fortunately, the injuries were not fatal on either side of the water, and there was no poison on the tips of the weapons to rankle in the wounds. Sensitive as most British writers are to the darts of transatlantic criticism, it has seemed to me sometimes that Mr. Lang is even tenderer of skin than are most of his fellow-sufferers.

The ocean that surges between Mr. Howells and Mr. Lang is unfordable, and there is no hope of a bridge. There is no common standing-ground anywhere for those who hold fiction to be primarily an amusement and those who believe that it ought to be chiefly a criticism of life, as Matthew Arnold said all literature should be. The romanticist considers fiction as an art, and as an art only ; whilst the extreme realist is inclined to look on it almost as a branch of science. Kindly as Mr. Lang may be in his reception of a realistic book, now and then, he stands firmly on the platform of the extreme romanticists. " Find forgetfulness of trouble, and taste the anodyne of dreams—that is what we desire " of a novel, he declares in his cordial essay on Dumas. And in another paper he calls again for a potion against insomnia :

" Pour out the nepenthe, in short, and I shall not ask if the cup be gold-chased by Mr. Stevenson, or a buffalo-horn beaker brought by Mr. Haggard from Kakuana-land—the Baron of Bradwardine's Bear, or ' The Cup of Hercules ' of Théophile Gautier, or merely a common café wine-glass of M. Fortuné du Boisgobey's or M. Xavier de Mon-

tépin's. If only the nepenthe be foaming there,—
the delightful draught of dear forgetfulness,—the
outside of the cup may take care of itself; or, to
drop metaphor, I shall not look too closely at an
author's manner and style, while he entertains me
in the dominion of dreams."

Here Mr. Lang is in accord with Mérimée,
who wrote in 1865 that "there is at present
but one man of genius : it is Ponson du Ter-
rail . . . No one handles crime as he does,
nor assassination. *J'en fais mes délices.*" But
Mérimée's humorous exaggeration is not in
accord with his own practice ; however abundant in imaginative vigour his stories might
be, nothing could be more rigorously realistic
in treatment. Mr. Lang seems to me happiest
as a story-teller when his practice departs from
his theory. His longest story, " The Mark of
Cain," is as who should say a tale by M. Xavier
de Montépin, but by a Montépin who was a
Scotsman, and had been to Oxford, and did
not take himself quite seriously. Now, for a
romanticist not to take himself seriously is to
give up the fight before the battle is joined.
Mr. Lang has balladed the praises of " Miss
Braddon and Gaboriau," and he may be sure
that these masters of sensation believed in
themselves, else would they never have held
thousands breathless. If an author once lets
his readers suspect that he is only "making
believe," instantly he loses his grip on their

attention, and may as well put away the
puppets, since few spectators will care to wait
till the fall of the curtain.

The one fault that Mr. James found with
Trollope—that "he took a suicidal satisfaction
in reminding the reader that the story he was
telling was only, after all, a make-believe"—
Mr. Lang never commits of malice prepense;
but though he does not confess this unpardonable sin in so many words, yet his tone, his
manner, his confidential approach, make the
confession for him, and readers find themselves glancing up from the printed page
to see if the author has not his tongue in
his cheek or is not laughing in his sleeve.
And the crime is the more heinous in story-
telling according to the romantic tradition
than in fiction of the realistic school. Mr.
James reminds us that "there are two kinds of
taste in the appreciation of imaginative literature ; the taste for emotions of surprise, and
the taste for emotions of recognition." It is
the latter that "Barchester Towers" gratifies,
and it is to the former that the "Mark of
Cain" appeals, and the taste for the emotion
of surprise is not satisfied if it suspects the
writer of treating tragic moments with levity,
or even of being capable of such treatment.
But perhaps the real reason why a public that
accepted the tawdry "Called Back" did not
take kindly to the "Mark of Cain" is that Mr.

Lang's story was too clever by half—a thing
resented by most of those who have a taste for
the emotion of surprise.

Perhaps the same criticism applies to some
of the stories in the collection called " In the
Wrong Paradise "—to the Poe-like tale of " A
Cheap Negro," for example. But others of
the stories in this volume, especially the un-
canny tales of spooks and of medicine-men,
are most delicious fooling — and fooling
founded on the impregnable rock of modern
science. What could be better in its way
than the " Great Gladstone Myth ? "—wherein
the grand old man is resolved into his elements in the fashion familiar to students of
sun-myths. Equally amusing, and quite as
pregnant in suggestion, is the description of
the poor souls who found themselves each " In
the Wrong Paradise "—the scalped Scotchman
dwelling with the Apaches in their happy
hunting-grounds, and the wretched cockney
esthete desperately out of place in the Fortunate Islands of the Greeks. And in the
volume of pleasant papers on " Books and
Bookmen " there is an eery tale of painful and
humorous misadventure in " A Bookman's
Purgatory." Akin to these in method, and
even superior to them in charm, is the story of
" Prince Prigio," which of all Mr. Lang's
fictions I like best, unhesitatingly proclaiming
it the most delightful of modern fairy tales

since the "Rose and the Ring;" and if any
one should tell me that he found no fun
in the awful combat between the Firedrake
and the Remora, I should make answer that
such an one, waking or sleeping, does not
deserve ever to receive as a gift, or even as a
loan, the seven-leagued boots, the cap of darkness, or the purse of Fortunatus—all properties of fairy-lore with which Prince Prigio was
duly accoutred.

From fairy-land to the doubtful region of
folklore is no seven-leagued stride, and Mr.
Lang is master in both territories. He stands
ready to trace the kinship of Barbarossa and
Barbe-bleue, and to insist that neither is a child
of the sun.   In defence of his theories Mr.
Lang is armed to give battle to Professor
Max Müller and his men; and they find him
a redoubtable opponent, in no danger of
putting off the heavy armour of scholarship
because he has not proved it, and never without a smooth stone in his scrip to cast full at
the forehead of his adversary.   Lowell has
protested against that zeal which seeks to explain away every myth as a personification of
the dawn and the day.   "There's not a sliver
left of Odin," he declared :

> "Or else the core his name enveloped
> Was from a solar myth developed
> Which, hunted to its primal shoot,
> Takes refuge in a Sanskrit root,

> Thereby to instant death explaining
> The little poetry remaining.
> Try it with Zeus, 't is just the same ;
> The thing evades, we hug a name ;
> Nay, scarcely that—perhaps a vapour
> Born of some atmospheric caper."

Against the philologic school of mytholo-
gists of whom Professor Max Müller is the
chief, Mr. Lang has led a revolt in behalf of an
anthropological explanation of those habits,
customs, beliefs, and legends for which the up-
holders of the sun-myth theory provided an
etymological interpretation.   Mr. Lecky tells
us that invariably with increased education the
belief in fairies passes away, and "from the
uniformity of this decline, we infer that fairy-
tales are the normal product of a certain condition of the imagination ; and this position is
raised to a moral certainty when we find that
the decline of fairy-tales is but one of a long
series of similar transformations."   Inspired
by McLennan and Professor Tylor, and following Fontenelle, Mr. Lang has given battle
to those who maintain that the descriptions of
the elemental processes of nature developed
into myths, and who accept a personification
of fire, storm, cloud, or lightning as the origin
of Apollo and his chariot, Thor and his ham-
mer, Cinderella and her slipper, and Brer
Rabbit and the tar-baby.

In the stead of the arbitrary interpretations

of the philologists, wherein scarcely any two of
them are agreed, Mr. Lang proffers an explanation derived from a study of the history
of man and founded on the methods of com-
parative anthropology. He turns to account
the evolution of humanity from savagery to
civilization, and he examines the irrational
beliefs and absurd customs which survived in
Greece even in the days of Pericles by the aid
of a study of the beliefs and customs of
savage tribes still in the condition in which the
ancient Greeks had once been. Thus he is
ready to see in the snake-dance of the Moquis
of Arizona a possible help to the right understanding of a similar ceremony described by
Demosthenes. He seeks to show that in
savagery we have " an historical condition
of the human intellect to which the element
in myths, regarded by us as irrational," seems
rational enough. Further, he urges that as
savagery is a stage through which all civilized
races have passed, the universality of the
mythopeic mental condition will explain not
only the origin, but also the diffusion throughout the world, of myths strangely alike one
to another.

That this ethnological hypothesis has gained
general acceptance, and placed the philologic
theory on the defensive, is due almost altogether to the untiring advocacy of Mr. Lang.
His views have been presented modestly but

firmly and incessantly.   He has prepared the
case himself, examined the witnesses, and
summed up for the plaintiff.   And he is an
awkward antagonist, quick-witted and keen-
sighted, and heavy-laden with the results of
original anthropological investigation.   He
has scholarship in the old sense of the word ;
and to this he adds the advantage of a memory
which retains every pertinent fact accumu-
lated during omnivorous reading over a marvellously wide range of subjects.   Most
disinterested scholars have now accepted
either as a whole or in part the theory
Mr. Lang has set forth.

Of the scholarship which forms the solid
basis for Mr. Lang's scientific inquiry he has
given abundant evidence in his nervous prose
translations of the " Odyssey " and the " Iliad "
done in partnership with friends, in his refined
rendering of the " Idyls " of Theocritus, and
in his fresh and fragrant version of that other
idyl, " Aucassin and Nicolette."   The trans-
fusion of a work of art from one language to
another is a feat of the utmost difficulty,
which Mr. Lang has accomplished with triumphant success, not only once or twice, but
thrice at least.   His translations reveal a most
unusual union of scholarly exactness with
idiomatic vigour ; they are graceful—almost
the rarest quality of a translation—and they
are unfailingly poetic.   Perhaps an enforced

quaintness, and an occasional insistence on an
archaic word, seem almost like affectation,
but this may be forgiven and forgotten in the
charm and the felicity of the rendering as a
whole. The secret of this charm is to be
found, I think, in Mr. Lang's attitude toward
the authors he translates. To him Homer,
and Theocritus, and the old man who sang of
" Aucassin and Nicolette," are still living,
and their works are alive. Scholar as he is,
his interest is never grammatical or linguistic,
but always literary and human. He never
regards these writings as verse to scan, or as
prose to parse, but poetry to be enjoyed.

As it happens, Mr. Lang has attempted no
long translations in verse, but some of his
briefer metrical attempts are almost as happy
as Longfellow's, than which there can hardly
be higher praise. No doubt the carrying
over of a lyric from one language to another
is an easier task than the transferring of an
epic, but nevertheless it is a feat many a
minor poet has failed to accomplish. The
difficulty lies in the double duty of the trans-
lator—to present the thought of his original
and to preserve the form, not sacrificing the
spirit, and at least suggesting the atmosphere.
Mr. Lang has given us the most satisfactory
version of Villon's " Ballade of Dead Ladies "
(although Rossetti attempted it earlier), and
of Clément Marot's "Brother Lubin" (although

both Longfellow and Bryant severally essayed
it, neglecting to retain the ballade form).

In his brightsome "Ballades in Blue China,"
and in his brilliant "Rhymes à la Mode,"
Mr. Lang shows his mastery of the accomplishment of verse, and his skill in that department of poetry which seems easy and is
beset with danger.   Voltaire tells us that
difficulty conquered in whatsoever form of art
is a large share of the merit ; and neither in
sonnet, nor ballade, nor other fixed form of
verse, has Mr. Lang shirked any difficulty. If
the game is worth the candle, Mrs. Battle is
right in insisting on the rigour of the game.
In his freer stanzas Mr. Lang has sometimes
something of the singing simplicity of Longfellow and Heine, where the music of the
verse sustains the emotion.   In " Twilight on
Tweed,"

> " A mist of memory broods and floats,
>   The Border waters flow :
> The air is full of ballad notes,
>   Borne out of long ago,"

and in " The Last Cast," the angler's thoughts
wander to the rivers he has never fished, and
then go back to the streams of Scotland
again :

> " Unseen, Eurotas, southward steal,
>   Unknown, Alpheus, westward glide,
> You never heard the ringing reel,
>   The music of the water-side !

" Though gods have walked your woods among,
    Though nymphs have fled your banks along,
You speak not that familiar tongue
    Tweed murmurs like my cradle song.

" My cradle song—nor other hymn
    I 'd choose, nor gentler requiem dear
Than Tweed's, that through death's twilight dim
    Mourned in the last Minstrel's ear."

Mr. Lang has taken for an epigraph
Molière's " Ce ne sont point de grands vers
pompeux, mais de petits vers," yet he has at
times the gift of lofty lines.   It is only fair to
judge a poet by his highest effort.   In the
case of the present poet these seem to me to
be two sonnets on Homer, of a sustained and
noble elevation.   For love of Homer's heroine
Mr. Lang has written his longest poem,
" Helen of Troy," a brevet-epic.

    " The face that launch'd a thousand ships
    And burnt the topless towers of Ilium "

holds its fascination still across the centuries.
Nor is " Sweet Helen," as Faustus calls her,
the only lady of Mr. Lang's affections.   He
has a wealth of platonic love for many a fair
dame (in poetry), and for many a damsel in
distress (in prose).   I doubt if he would deny
his devotion to Beatrix Esmond, for whose
sake the author of " The Faithful Fool," a
comedy once performed by Her Majesty's

Servants, broke his sword before his king. I
question whether he would not admit an affection for Mrs. Rawdon Crawley, *née* Sharp, a
green-eyed lady who once acted Clytemnestra
at the Gaunt House theatricals. I know that
he confesses a fondness for Manon Lescaut, a
young person of reprehensible morals, who
lightly sinned in France and then died happily
in Louisiana. And I think that he is ready
to boast of his liking for Miss Annie P. Miller
of Schenectady, New York, an American girl
who was known to her intimates as " Daisy,"
and who died in Rome after an imprudent
visit to the Colosseum by moonlight.

Mr. Lang has the same frank and sturdy
love for literature that he has for some of its
captivating female figures. No reader of his
could be in doubt as to his ceaseless and loyal
study of Homer and Theocritus, of Rabelais
and Molière, of Shakespeare and Thackeray.
And in sports, too, his tastes are as wholesome
and as abundant as his predilections in letters.
He cherishes the cricket of Oxford and the
golf of St. Andrews ; he follows with equal
zest trout-fishing and book-hunting. Than
this last there is indeed no better sport ; and
the poetic author of " Books and Bookmen "
has proved his interest in the bees of De
Thou as well as in those that made the honey
of Hymettus. The original Crichton, we
may remember, sent an epistle in verse to

Aldus Manutius, the great printer-publisher of Venice.

Mr. Lang is at his best when he writes about the Scots and about the Greeks of old, for these he knows and loves ; and perhaps he appears to least advantage when he is writing about the American writers of to-day, since these he neither likes nor cares to know—and unsympathetic criticism is foredoomed to sterility. The native Americans Mr. Lang is most familiar with are the red men, and he is fonder of them, I fancy, than he is of the pale faces who have built towns by the banks of the streams over which Uncas and Hard-Heart skilfully propelled their birch-bark canoes. It might have been better, therefore, had he not laid himself open to Mr. Fiske's rebuke for the "impatient contempt" with which he chose to speak of a man of Lewis H. Morgan's calibre ; and if he had not permitted himself his recent and doubtfully courteous attack on Mr. Boyesen. And a more careful understanding of American literary history would have saved Mr. Lang from that farewell to Poe, in the "Letters to Dead Authors," in which the author of "The Raven" is hailed as "a gentleman among *canaille !*"—surely as strange an opinion as one can find in all the long annals of criticism.

"Letters to Dead Authors" is one of the minor masterpieces of letters, the keenest and

cleverest volume of playful criticism since the
"Fable for Critics" was published two-score
years ago, as that in its turn was the brightest
book of the kind since "Rejected Addresses."
But I am afraid to linger over this delightful
tome for fear I may laud it extravagantly.
The "Epistle to Mr. Alexander Pope," a
marvel of parody with many lines as good as
the one which tells the poet that "Dunces
edit him whom dunces feared!"—the letter to
"Monsieur de Molière, Valet-de-Chambre du
Roi," with its delicious suggestion that if the
great and sad French humorist were alive
to-day, he might write a new comedy on *les
Moliéristes;*—the communication to Herodotus,
with its learned fooling;—the missive to
Alexandre Dumas, with its full current of
hearty admiration and enjoyment;—these and
many another I dare not dwell on, because, as
I read in the letter to W. M. Thackeray,
"there are many things that stand in the way
of the critic when he has a mind to praise the
living." Quite as welcome as these are some
of the essays in epistolary parody to be found
in "Old Friends."

Of necessity every man has the defects of
his qualities, and the very success of Mr.
Lang's briefer essays tends to prevent his
attempting longer labours. He gets most out
of a subject which may be treated on the
instalment plan, when every portion is com-

plete in itself, and yet unites with the others
to form a complete whole.   A book like
" Letters to Dead Authors," which is avowedly
a collection of separable essays, has not only
a broader outlook but also a stronger unity
than the pleasantly discursive volume on
Oxford, for example. A collection of Tanagra
figurines, however, is in no wise inferior in
interest to a colossal statue ; art has nothing
to do with mere bulk, nor has literature.
Mr. Lang cultivates to best advantage ground
which can most easily be cut into allotments.

It is to be noted also that despite his
extreme multifariousness there are certain
segments of life and of literature in which Mr.
Lang takes little interest or none. Though
he once wrote a poem on General Gordon,
and though he is ever chaffing Mr. Gladstone,
it is obvious that he cares not for the contentions of politics ; and apparently he cares
as little for the disputes of theology, although
he did write a chance article on " Robert
Elsmere."   For art, music, and the drama he
reveals no natural inclination. We may guess
that it has been his fate to serve as art-critic,
toiling in the galleries yearly ; but we can
discover no signs of any real understanding of
art, either pictorial or plastic, nor of any
aptitude for it. Of music he says almost
nothing, and he seems to know as little about
it as we know about the song the Syrens

sang.   And as for the acted drama, I am
afraid that he is a heretic, even as Lamb was
heretical in regard to the performance of
Shakespeare's plays.   I hesitate to assert,
though I am inclined to believe, that to him
" As You Like It " and " Much Ado About
Nothing " are comedies to be read in the
fields or by the fire-side, rather than stage-
plays to be acted before the footlights.

Nor has he busied himself with any science
other than anthropology.   But what of it?
His interests are wider than those of almost
any other man of letters in our time ; and in
these days, when the pressure of civilization
forces men into an entreme and cramping
specialization, Mr. Lang has circumvented
this tendency by cultivating not one speciality
or two, but a dozen at least.   And perhaps
there could be no better proof of his surpassing cleverness.

1893.

II. MR. ROBERT LOUIS STEVENSON.

THE news of the death of Robert Louis
Stevenson in that far-off Pacific isle,
removed by half a continent from his native
Scotland, gave a sudden shock to all who
care for our later literature ; and it left us, I
think, with a sense of personal loss, as though
he had died with whom we had held delightful
intercourse in the past, and with whom we
could hope to have many another stimulating
talk in the future. This feeling was doubled
and far deeper in those of us who had the
privilege of knowing Stevenson, even if our
acquaintance with him were as slight as mine
—and I can treasure the precious memory of
but a single long afternoon on the same sofa
with him, in the dingy back smoking-room of
the Savile Club, one dismal day of a London
summer nearly ten years ago. Chiefly we
talked of our craft, of the art of story-telling,
of the technic of play-making. I remember
distinctly his hearty praise of Mark Twain's
" Huckleberry Finn," and his cordial belief
that it was a great book, riper in art and

M

ethically richer than the "Tom Sawyer" of which it is the sequel. I recall the courtesy and the frankness with which he gave me his opinion of a tale of mine he happened to have read recently. Frankness, indeed, was a constant quality of his conversation ; and perhaps his spoken word was fresher and freer than his written lines—it could not but be less premeditated. With a very strong individuality, there was no pose in his manner, no affectation, no airs and graces. He looked unlike other men, with his tall thin figure, his long thin face, his nervous thin hands. As one's eyes first fell on him one felt that he was somebody, and not anybody at random. If one had dropped into talk with him by chance in a train or in a doctor's waiting-room, one could not have resisted the impress of his personality. He talked well, although not perhaps with the spontaneous many-sidedness of his friend Fleeming Jenkin (whom he introduced as Cockshot in his own essay on "Talk and Talkers"). He talked well, standing up squarely against the other party to the conversation, holding his own stoutly, expressing his views in straightforward fashion, with no beating about the bush, no questing of epigram, no strain of phrase-making. He talked well, as he wrote well, because he had something to say, and because he had taught himself how best to say it.

In the writing of the author, as in the talk of the man himself, perhaps the two salient qualities were vigour and variety. The vigour everyone has felt who chances to have read a single book of Stevenson's—and who of us, having read any one of them, has not sat himself down to read them all? The variety is equally evident if we look down the long list of his works—and the list is really very long indeed, when we remember that the books on it were written, all of them, by a dying man, who finally departed this life before he was fifty. He was a poet of distinction, although not of high achievement. Although no single one of his poems has been taken home to the hearts of the people of his speech, yet "A Child's Garden of Verses" is as unlike any rhymes of earlier poets as any volume of verse of this last quarter of the nineteenth century. He was a writer of travel sketches, and here again he revealed the same originality; and he was able to describe "Edinburgh," his boyhood's home, with the same freedom from staleness, the same eschewal of the commonplace, that gave freshness to "Silverado Squatters;" while in "Travels with a Donkey and "An Inland Voyage" he achieved a detachment of the man from his circumstances unattempted by anybody before, excepting only the author of "Walden." He was a biographer and a literary critic, and although

his life of "Fleeming Jenkin" is the least successful of his works, being marred by a hint
of a patronizing manner entirely unbecoming
toward a man of the character and accomplishment of "The Flamer," still the task was done
in workmanlike fashion ; and Stevenson's
other sketches of authors in his "Familiar
Studies of Men and Books," and elsewhere,
are free from this defect. It is to be noted
here that he was one of the rare British critics
capable of appreciating Walt Whitman with
sanity, while another American, Thoreau, was
perhaps almost the strongest of all the in-
fluences which moulded him — quite the
strongest after Scott. He was an essayist,
and among the most piquant and individual
of his time, an essayist of the race and lineage
of Montaigne, of Lamb, and of Lowell, interested in life as much as in literature, seeing
for himself, always inquiring and always ac-
quisitive, having philosophical standards of
his own, and using them to measure men and
manners, and yet never intolerant, though ever
sincere. He was a dramatist, at least one of
whose plays, "Deacon Brodie," was fairly successful in withstanding the touchstone test of
the actual theatre ; yet it must be admitted
that his dramas, written, all of them, in con-
junction with Mr. W. E. Henley, have rather
the robustious manner of that burly writer
than the commingled delicacy and force of

Stevenson's other work.   And, lastly, he was
also a story-teller.

It is as a story-teller that he won his widest
triumphs ; it is as a story-teller that he is
most likely to linger on the shelves of our
grandchildren's libraries ; it was as a story-
teller that he revealed his greatest variety.
First and last he tried his hand at four kinds
of fiction.   In the " New Arabian Nights,"
with its sequel, the " Dynamiter," he revived
the tale of fantasy with an inventive ingenuity
unequalled certainly since Poe published the
" Tales of the Grotesque and the Arabesque."
In the " Strange Case of Dr. Jekyll and Mr.
Hyde," and in " Markheim," he gave us the
strongest stories of introspection and imagination since Hawthorne's " Scarlet Letter " and
" Marble Faun."   In " Kidnapped " and in
" David Balfour " and in the " Master of Bal-
lantrae " he presented us with the most vivid
and actual of Scotch romances since Scott
came home from vacant exile to die at Abbots-
ford.   And in " The Wrecker " and certain of
its fellows he tried, not without a large measure
of success, to varnish with sheer art the vulgar
detective story, and to give a tincture of literature to the tale of crime committed and of
secrets ferreted out at last.   And even now,
though it has been easy to show that as a
teller of tales Stevenson's versatility has thus
four phases, " Treasure Island " has to be left

out of the account, simply because it refuses
to classify itself with the others, perhaps
because it prefers to take its chances with
" Robinson Crusoe."

Stevenson had his theory of fiction, and his
practice was like his preaching—which is
another proof of his originality.   In the evolution of the modern novel from the primitive
romance, in the progress first from the Impossible to the Improbable, and then from the
Probable to the Inevitable, he refused to go
to the end.

He preferred the Improbable to the Inevitable.   He was a romanticist to the backbone,
a reactionary, so those of us think who most
relish in literature the essence of actual life.
But though he fought for his own hand, and
defended his own doctrine stanchly, with characteristic good faith he tried to understand
the point of view of those with whom he con-
tended.   Himself liking the dramatic novel,
as he called it, the bold romance wherein is
set forth the strife of passionate character
against passionate character, he did not approve of Mr. Henry James's habit of keeping
the *scène-à-faire* behind closed doors.   Yet in
his reply to Mr. James's paper on the " Art of
Fiction," a reply which he modestly entitled
" A Humble Remonstrance," he combated the
views of the author of "Daisy Miller" with
the utmost courtesy ; and in a postscript to

the same paper he dissented from what he
called the "narrow convictions" of Mr.
Howells; but he seized the occasion to declare the author of "Silas Lapham" to be "a
poet, a finished artist, a man in love with the
appearance of life, a cunning reader of the
mind."

Being a Scotsman, Stevenson was nearer to
the American than the Englishman can be,
and he had a quicker willingness to understand the American character. As a Scotsman, also, he had keener artistic perceptions
than an Englishman is likely to have. He
was not only a born story-teller, as Scott was,
but he was also a master of the craft, a loving,
devoted, untiring student of the art, which
Scott was not. He never attained to the
mastery of form which Guy de Maupassant
derived as a tradition from the French classics;
his stories are often straggling. And he had
not the relish for fresh technicalities which is
one of Mr. Rudyard Kipling's peculiarities. I
remember Fleeming Jenkin's telling me how
his sons, who had sailed a boat from their
earliest youth, were sorely puzzled by the impossible manœuvres of the ship in "Treasure
Island," and how they came to their father de-
spairingly to declare that "this never happened,
did it? It couldn't, could it?"

Not only these deficiencies have been dwelt
on, but the absence has been pointed out of

what is known as the "female interest" in his
stories; and it is a fact that almost the only
satisfactory and enticing petticoats of Mr.
Stevenson's draping are in "David Balfour."
But these defects are as naught against the
narrative skill of Stevenson, his unfailing fertility of invention, his firm grasp of character,
his insight into the springs of human nature,
and, above all, his contagious interest in the
tale he is telling.

Whether it is a tale he is telling, or a drama
with its swift sharp dialogue, or an essay ram-
bling and ambling skilfully to its unseen end,
the style is always the style of a man who has
learnt how to make words bend to his bidding.
He writes as one whom the parts of speech
must needs obey. He had a picked vocabulary at his command, and he was ever on the
watch for the unexpected phrase. He strove
incessantly to escape from the hackneyed form
of words, and cut-and-dried commonplaces of
speech—and no doubt the effort is evident
sometimes, although the instances are rare
enough. There is at times, it is true, more
than a hint of preciousness, but he never fell
into the self-consciousness which marred many
of the late Mr. Walter Pater's periods. "Prince
Otto," written obviously under the influence of
Mr. George Meredith, had more of these ani-
line patches, as it was also the feeblest of his
fictions. "The Open Letter on Father Damien,"

for example, had a sturdy directness of statement which suggested Walt Whitman again.

The impression of mere dilettante idling which one may get at first from some of the earlier essays is evanescent. As Mr. James put it, much as Stevenson " cares for his phrase, he cares more for life, and for a certain transcendently lovable part of it." And herein Mr. James saw " the respectable, desirable moral." To me, at least, there was no need to seek a moral between the lines, for was not Stevenson a true Scotsman, and could he ever forget the chief end of man? Only a Scotsman could have written the " Strange Case of Dr. Jekyll and Mr. Hyde," as only a New Englander could have written the " Scarlet Letter." There is an inheritance from the Covenanters and a memory of the Shorter Catechism in Stevenson's bending and twisting the dark problems of our common humanity to serve as the core of his tales.

It is curious that a writer so independent as Stevenson and so various should have been tempted so often into collaboration ; but it is a fact that no man of letters of our time and our language has taken more literary partners. With Mr. W. E. Henley he composed at least four plays, and they are set down rather to Mr. Henley's credit, I think, than to Stevenson's. With Mrs. Stevenson he wrote the " Dynamiter ; " and with her son, Mr. Lloyd

Osbourne, he told three tales, the "Wrong Box," the "Wrecker," and the "Ebb-Tide," in which we find a more open humour than in his other stories. But, as those only know who have themselves collaborated in good faith, it is always impossible to disentangle the contribution of one partner from that of the other, if, indeed, there has been not a mere mechanical mixture, but a true chemical union. Whatever associates Stevenson had now and again, he was the senior partner always, and it was his trade-mark that warranted the goods of the firm.

Long as the list is of the books Stevenson published since "Edinburgh" appeared in 1878, he left much of his writing scattered here and there. To say nothing of chance articles in the "Academy" and elsewhere, and of more important papers in the British monthly reviews, including a most interesting essay on "Style," and a most suggestive inquiry as to the future of mankind, there is another play, "Robert Macaire," written for Mr. Henry Irving, but never produced. There is another boy story, never reprinted from the pages of the juvenile weekly in which "Treasure Island" and the "Black Arrow" appeared. There are the letters on "The South Seas : a Record of Three Cruises," published in newspapers both in Great Britain and the United States, but perhaps not to be sent forth by

themselves.   There are two of his strongest
short stories, " Markheim " and the " Body-
Snatcher," waiting to be included in some
volume of brief tales.   And there are certain
firstlings of his art, the pamphlet on the
" Pentland Rising, a Page of History, 1666,"
and the " Charity Bazar, an Allegorical Dialogue," both of which are said to be included
in the new and uniform edition of all his
works, the earlier of the volumes of which had
but just appeared when he died.   Probably
the story once announced as the " Jail-Bird "
is that which has been published as the " Ebb-
Tide."   Fortunately he did not die leaving
behind him a novel half published and half
finished, as Thackeray did and Hawthorne.
And it is little likely that anything that may
appear posthumously will either enlarge his
reputation or detract from it.   For his fame
is secure, and the corner-stones of it are the
" New Arabian Nights " and " Kidnapped,"
" Treasure Island," and the " Strange Case of
Dr. Jekyll and Mr. Hyde."

1894.

THE CENTENARY OF FENIMORE COOPER.

MOST appropriate is it that the first
literary centenary which we were called
upon to commemorate one hundred years after
the adoption of the Constitution that knit these
States into a nation should be the birthday of
the author who has done the most to make us
known to the nations of Europe.   In the first
year of Washington's first term as President,
on the fifteenth day of September, 1789, was
born James Fenimore Cooper, the first of
American novelists, and the first American
author to carry our flag outside the limits of
our language.   Franklin was the earliest
American who had fame among foreigners;
but his wide popularity was due rather to his
achievements as a philosopher, as a physicist,
as a statesman, than to his labours as an
author.   Irving was six years older than
Cooper, and his reputation was as high in
England as at home; yet to this day he is
little more than a name to those who do not
speak our mother-tongue.   But after Cooper
had published " The Spy," " The Last of the

Mohicans," and "The Pilot" his popularity
was cosmopolitan ; he was almost as widely
read in France, in Germany, and in Italy as
in Great Britain and the United States. Only
one American book has ever since attained
the international success of these of Cooper's
—" Uncle Tom's Cabin ;" and only one American author has since gained a name at all com-
mensurate with Cooper's abroad—Poe. Here
in these United States we know what Emerson was to us and what he did for us and what
our debt is to him ; but the French and the
Germans and the Italians do not know Emerson. When Mr. Boyesen visited Hugo some
ten years ago he found that the great French
lyrist had never heard of Emerson. I happen
to have a copy of " Evangeline " annotated in
French for the use of French children learn-
ing English at school ; but whatever Longfellow's popularity in England or in Germany,
he is really but little known in France or Italy
or Spain. With Goethe and Schiller, with
Scott and Byron, Cooper was one of the
foreign forces which brought about the Romanticist revolt in France, profoundly affecting the
literature of all Latin countries. Dumas owed
almost as much to Cooper as he did to Scott;
and Balzac said that if Cooper had only drawn
character as well as he painted " the phenomena of nature, he would have uttered the last
word of our art."

In his admirable life of Cooper, one of the best of modern biographies, Professor Louns- bury shows clearly the extraordinary state of affairs with which Cooper had to contend. Foremost among the disadvantages against which he had to labour was the dull, deaden- ing provincialism of American criticism at the time when " The Spy " was written ; and as we read Professor Lounsbury's pages we see how bravely Cooper fought for our intellectual emancipation from the shackles of the British criticism of that time, more ignorant then and even more insular than it is now. Abroad Cooper received the attention nearly always given in literature to those who bring a new thing ; and the new thing which Cooper an- nexed to literature was America. At home he had to struggle against a belief that our soil was barren of romance—as though the author who used his eyes could not find ample material wherever there was humanity. Cooper was the first who proved the fitness of Ameri- can life and American history for the uses of fiction. " The Spy " is almost the earliest of American novels, and it remains one of the best. Cooper was the prospector of that little army of industrious miners now engaged in working every vein of local colour and character, and in sifting out the golden dust from the sands of local history. The authors of " Oldtown Folks," of the " Tales of the

Argonauts," of "Old Creole Days," and of
" In the Tennessee Mountains " were but following in Cooper's footsteps—though they
carried more modern tools.   And when the
desire of the day is for detail and for finish, it
is not without profit to turn again to stories of
a bolder sweep.   When the tendency of the
times is perhaps towards an undue elabora-
tion of miniature portraits, there is gain in
going back to the masterpieces of a literary
artist who succeeded best in heroic statues.
And not a few of us, whatever our code of
literary esthetics, may find delight, fleeting
though it be, in the free outline drawing of
Cooper, after our eyes are tired by the niggling
and cross-hatching of many among our contemporary realists.   When our pleasant duty
is done, when our examination is at an end,
and when we seek to sum up our impressions
and to set them down plainly, we find that
chief among Cooper's characteristics were, first,
a sturdy, hearty, robust, out-door and open-air
wholesomeness, devoid of any trace of offence
and free from all morbid taint ; and, secondly,
an intense Americanism—ingrained, abiding,
and dominant.   Professor Lounsbury quotes
from a British magazine of 1831 the statement that, to an Englishman, Cooper appeared
to be prouder of his birth as an American than
of his genius as an author—an attitude which
may seem to some a little old-fashioned, but

which on Cooper's part was both natural and becoming.

"The Spy" was the earliest of Cooper's American novels (and its predecessor, "Precaution," a mere stencil imitation of the minor British novel of that day, need not be held in remembrance against him). "The Spy," published in 1821, was followed in 1823 by "The Pioneers," the first of the "Leatherstocking Tales" to appear, and by far the poorest ; indeed it is the only one of the five for which any apology need be made. The narrative drags under the burden of overabundant detail ; and the story may deserve to be called dull at times. Leatherstocking even is but a faint outline of himself, as the author afterwards with loving care elaborated the character. "The Last of the Mohicans" came out in 1826, and its success was instantaneous and enduring. In 1827 appeared "The Prairie," the third tale in which Leatherstocking is the chief character. It is rare that an author is ever able to write a successful sequel to a successful story, yet Cooper did more ; "The Prairie" is a sequel to "The Pioneers," and "The Last of the Mohicans" is a prologue to it. Eighteen years after the first of the "Leatherstocking Tales" had been published, Cooper issued the last of them, amplifying his single sketch into a drama in five acts by the addition of "The Pathfinder"

printed in 1840, and of " The Deerslayer,"
printed in 1841. In the sequence of events
" The Deerslayer," the latest written, is the
earliest to be read ; then comes " The Last of
the Mohicans," followed by " The Pathfinder "
and " The Pioneers ; " while in " The Prairie "
the series ends. Of the incomparable variety
of scene in these five related tales, or of the
extraordinary fertility of invention which they
reveal, it would not be easy to say too much.
In their kind they have never been surpassed.
The earliest to appear, " The Pioneers," is the
least meritorious—as though Cooper had not
yet seen the value of his material, and had not
yet acquired the art of handling it to advantage. " The Pathfinder," dignified as it is and
pathetic in its portrayal of Leatherstocking's
love-making, lacks the absorbing interest of
" The Last of the Mohicans ; " it is perhaps
inferior in art to " The Deerslayer " which was
written the year after, and it has not the
noble simplicity of " The Prairie," in which we
see the end of the old hunter.

There are, no doubt, irregularities in the
" Leatherstocking Tales," and the incongruities
and lesser errors inevitable in a mode of com-
position at once desultory and protracted ;
but there they stand, a solid monument of
American literature, and not the least enduring. "If anything from the pen of the
writer of these romances is at all to outlive

N

himself, it is, unquestionably, the series of the
" Leatherstocking Tales"—so wrote the author
when he sent forth the first collected and
revised edition of the narrative of Natty
Bumppo's adventures.   That Cooper was
right seems to-day indisputable.   An author
may fairly claim to be judged by his best,
to be measured by his highest; and the
" Leatherstocking Tales " are Cooper's highest
and best in more ways than one, but chiefly
because of the lofty figure of Leatherstocking.
Lowell, when fabling for critics, said that
Cooper had drawn but one new character, explaining afterwards that

" The men who have given to *one* character life
And objective existence, are not very rife ;
You may number them all, both prose-writers and
    singers,
Without overrunning the bounds of your fingers ;
And Natty won't go to oblivion quicker
Than Adams the parson or Primrose the vicar."

And   Thackeray — perhaps   recalling   the
final scene in " The Prairie," where the dying
Leatherstocking drew himself up and said
" Here ! " and that other scene in " The New-
comes," where the dying Colonel drew himself
up and said " Adsum ! "—was frequent in praise
of Cooper ; and in one of the " Roundabout
Papers," after expressing his fondness for Scott's
modest and honourable heroes, he adds :

"Much as I like these most unassuming, manly, unpretentious gentlemen, I have to own that I think the heroes of another writer—viz., Leatherstocking, Uncas, Hardheart, Tom Coffin—are quite the equals of Scott's men; perhaps Leatherstocking is better than any one in 'Scott's lot.' 'La Longue Carabine' is one of the great prize-men of fiction. He ranks with your Uncle Toby, Sir Roger de Coverley, Falstaff—heroic figures all, American or British, and the artist has deserved well of his country who devised them."

It is to be noticed that Thackeray singled out for praise two of Cooper's Indians to pair with the hunter and the sailor; and it seems to me that Thackeray is fairer towards him who conceived Uncas and Hardheart than are the authors of "A Fable for Critics" and of "Condensed Novels." "Muck-a-Muck" I should set aside among the parodies which are unfair—so far as the red man is concerned, at least; for I hold as quite fair Mr. Harte's raillery of the wooden maidens and polysyllabic old men who stalk through Cooper's pages. Cooper's "Indian" has been disputed and he has been laughed at, but he still lives. Cooper's Indian is very like Parkman's Indian—and who knew the red man better than the author of "The Oregon Trail?" Uncas and Chingachgook and Hardheart are all good men and true, and June, the wife of Arrowhead, the Tuscarora, is a good wife and

a true woman. They are Indians, all of them ;
heroic figures, no doubt, and yet taken from
life, with no more idealization than may serve
the maker of romance. They remind us that
when West first saw the Apollo Belvedere he
thought at once of a Mohawk brave. They
were the result of knowledge and of much
patient investigation under conditions forever
passed away. We see Cooper's Indians nowadays through mists of prejudice due to those
who have imitated them from the outside.
" The Last of the Mohicans " has suffered the
degradation of a trail of dime novels, written
by those apparently more familiar with the
Five Points than with the Five Nations ;
Cooper begat Mayne Reid, and Mayne Reid
begat Ned Buntline and " Buffalo Bill's First
Scalp for Custer " and similar abominations.
But none the less are Uncas and Hardheart
noble figures, worthily drawn, and never to be
mentioned without praise.

In 1821 Cooper published " The Spy," the
first American historical novel ; in 1823 he
published " The Pioneers," in which the back-
woodsman and the red man were first introduced into literature ; and in 1824 he published " The Pilot," and for the first time the
scene of a story was laid on the sea rather
than on the land, and the interest turned
wholly on marine adventure. In four years
Cooper had put forth three novels, each in its

way road-breaking and epoch-making : only the great men of letters have a record like this. With the recollection before us of some of Smollett's highly coloured naval characters, we cannot say that Cooper sketched the first real sailor in fiction, but he invented the sea-tale just as Poe invented the detective-story—and in neither case has any disciple surpassed the master. The supremacy of the " The Pilot " and " The Red Rover " is quite as evident as the supremacy of the " The Gold Bug " and " The Murders in the Rue Morgue." We have been used to the novel of the ocean, and it is hard for us now to understand why Cooper's friends thought his attempt to write one perilous and why they sought to dissuade him. It was believed that readers could not be interested in the contingencies and emergencies of life on the ocean wave. Nowadays it seems to us that if any part of " The Pilot " lags and stumbles it is that which passes ashore : Cooper's landscapes, or at least his views of a ruined abbey, may be affected at times, but his marines are always true and always captivating.

Cooper, like Thackeray, forbade his family to authorize or aid any biographer—although the American novelist had as little to conceal as the British. No doubt Cooper had his faults, both as a man and as an author. He was thin-skinned and hot-headed. He let himself become involved in a great many foolish quarrels. He had a plentiful lack of tact. But the man was straightforward and high-minded, and so was the author. We can readily pardon his petty pedantries and the little vices of expression he persisted in. We can confess that his "females," as he would term them, are indubitably wooden. We may acknowlege that even among his men there is no wide range of character; Richard Jones (in "The Pioneers") is first cousin to Cap (in "The Pathfinder"), just as Long Tom Coffin is a half-brother of Natty Bumppo. We must admit that Cooper's lighter characters are not touched with the humour that Scott could command at will; the Naturalist (in "The Prairie"), for example, is not alive and delightful like the "Antiquary" of Scott.

In the main, indeed, Cooper's humour is not of the purest. When he attempted it of malice prepense it was often laboriously unfunny. But sometimes, as it fell accidentally from the lips of Leatherstocking, it was unforced and delicious (see, for instance, at the end of chapter xxvii. of "The Pathfinder," the account of Natty's sparing the sleeping Mingos and of the fate which thereafter befell them at the hands of Chingachgook). On the other hand, Cooper's best work abounds in

fine romantic touches—Long Tom pinning
the British captain to the mast with the har-
poon, the wretched Abiram (in " The Prairie ")
tied hand and foot and left on a ledge with a
rope around his neck so that he can move
only to hang himself, the death-grip of the
brave (in " The Last of the Mohicans ") hang-
ing wounded and without hope over the
watery abyss :—these are pictures fixed in the
memory and now unforgetable.

Time is unerring in its selection. Cooper
has now been dead nearly two-score years.
What survives of his work are the " Sea Tales "
and the " Leatherstocking Tales." From these
I have found myself forced to cite characters
and episodes. These are the stories which
hold their own in the libraries. Public and
critics are at one here. The wind of the lakes
and the prairies has not lost its balsam, and
the salt of the sea keeps its savour. For the
free movement of his figures and for the
proper expansion of his story Cooper needed
a broad region and a widening vista. He
excelled in conveying the suggestion of vast-
ness and limitless space, and of depicting the
human beings proper to these great reaches
of land and water—the two elements he ruled ;
and he was equally at home on the rolling
waves of the prairie and on the green and
irregular hillocks of the ocean.

1889.

DISSOLVING VIEWS.

I. OF MARK TWAIN'S BEST STORY.

THE boy of to-day is fortunate indeed, and, of a truth, he is to be congratulated. While the boy of yesterday had to stay his stomach with the unconscious humour of "Sandford and Merton," the boy of to-day may get his fill of fun and of romance and of adventure in the "Story of a Bad Boy," in "Treasure Island," in "Tom Brown," and in "Tom Sawyer," and then in the sequel to "Tom Sawyer," wherein Tom himself appears in the very nick of time, like a young god from the machine. Sequels of stories which have been widely popular are not a little risky. "Huckleberry Finn" is a sharp exception to the general rule of failure. Although it is a sequel, it is quite as worthy of wide popularity as "Tom Sawyer." An American critic once neatly declared that the late G. P. R. James hit the bull's-eye of success with his first shot, and that forever thereafter he went on firing through the same hole. Now this is just what Mark Twain has not done : "Huckle-

berry Finn" is not an attempt to do "Tom
Sawyer" over again.   It is a story quite as
unlike its predecessor as it is like.   Although
Huck Finn appeared first in the earlier book,
and although Tom Sawyer reappears in the
later, the scenes and the characters are otherwise wholly different.   Above all, the atmosphere of the story is different.   "Tom
Sawyer" was a tale of boyish adventure in a
village in Missouri, on the Mississippi River,
and it was told by the author.   "Huckleberry
Finn" is autobiographic ; it is a tale of boyish
adventure along the Mississippi River told as
it appeared to Huck Finn.   There is not in
"Huckleberry Finn" any one scene quite as
funny as those in which Tom Sawyer gets his
friends to whitewash the fence for him, and
then uses the spoils thereby acquired to attain
the highest distinction of the Sunday-school
the next morning.   Nor is there any situation
quite as thrilling as that awful moment in the
cave when the boy and the girl are lost in the
darkness ; and when Tom Sawyer suddenly
sees a human hand bearing a light, and then
finds that the hand is the hand of Indian Joe,
his one mortal enemy   I have always thought
that the vision of the hand in the cave in
"Tom Sawyer" was one of the very finest
things in the literature of adventure since
Robinson Crusoe first saw a single footprint
in the sand of the sea-shore.

But though "Huckleberry Finn" may not
quite reach these two highest points of "Tom
Sawyer," the general level of the later story is
indisputably higher than that of the earlier.
For one thing, the skill with which the character of Huck Finn is maintained is marvellous. We see everything through his eyes ;
—and they are his eyes, and not a pair of
Mark Twain's spectacles. And the comments
on what he sees are his comments—the comments of an ignorant, superstitious, sharp,
healthy boy, brought up as Huck Finn had
been brought up ; they are not speeches put
into his mouth by the author. One of the
most artistic things in the book—and that
Mark Twain is a literary artist of a very high
order all who have considered his later writings
critically cannot but confess—one of the most
artistic things in "Huckleberry Finn" is the
sober self-restraint with which Mr. Clemens
lets Huck Finn set down, without any comment at all, scenes which would have afforded
the ordinary writer matter for endless moral
and political and sociological disquisition. I
refer particularly to the accounts of the Grangerford-Shepherdson feud, and of the shooting
of Boggs by Colonel Sherburn. Here are two
incidents of the rough old life of the South-
western States and of the Mississippi Valley,
forty or fifty years ago, of the old life which
is now rapidly passing away under the in-

fluence of advancing civilization and increasing commercial prosperity, but which has not wholly disappeared even yet, although a slow revolution in public sentiment is taking place. The Grangerford-Shepherdson feud is a vendetta as deadly as any Corsican could wish, yet the parties to it were honest, brave, sincere, good Christian people, probably people of deep religious sentiment.   None the less we see them taking their guns to church, and, when occasion serves, joining in what is little better than a general massacre.   The killing of Boggs by Colonel Sherburn is told with equal sobriety and truth ; and the later scene in which Colonel Sherburn cows and lashes the mob which has set out to lynch him is one of the most vigorous bits of writing Mark Twain has done.

In "Tom Sawyer" we saw Huckleberry Finn from the outside ; in the present volume we see him from the inside.   He is almost as much a delight to any one who has been a boy as was Tom Sawyer.   But only he or she who has been a boy can truly enjoy this record of his adventures and of his sentiments and of his sayings.   Old maids of either sex will wholly fail to understand him, or to like him, or to see his significance and his value. Like Tom Sawyer, Huck Finn is a genuine boy ; he is neither a girl in boy's clothes, like many of the modern heroes of juvenile fiction, nor is he a " little man," a full-grown man cut down ; he is a boy, just a boy, only a boy. And his ways and modes of thought are boyish. As Mr. F. Anstey understands the English boy, and especially the English boy of the middle classes, so Mark Twain understands the American boy, and especially the American boy of the Mississippi Valley of forty or fifty years ago. The contrast between Tom Sawyer, who is the child of respectable parents, decently brought up, and Huckleberry Finn, who is the child of the town drunkard, not brought up at all, is made distinct by a hundred artistic touches, not the least natural of which is Huck's constant reference to Tom as his ideal of what a boy should be. When Huck escapes from the cabin where his drunken and worthless father had confined him, carefully manufacturing a mass of very circumstantial evidence to prove his own murder by robbers, he cannot help saying, " I did wish Tom Sawyer was there ; I knowed he would take an interest in this kind of business, and throw in the fancy touches. Nobody could spread himself like Tom Sawyer in such a thing as that." Both boys have their full share of boyish imagination ; and Tom Sawyer, being given to books, lets his imagination run on robbers and pirates, having a perfect understanding with himself that, if you want to get fun out of this life, you must never hesitate to

make believe very hard ; and, with Tom's
youth and health, he never finds it hard to
make believe and to be a pirate at will, or to
summon an attendant spirit, or to rescue a
prisoner from the deepest dungeon 'neath the
castle moat.   But in Huck this imagination
has turned to superstition ; he is a walking
repository of the juvenile folk-lore of the
Mississippi Valley—a folk-lore partly traditional among the white settlers, but largely
influenced by intimate association with the
negroes.   When Huck was in his room at
night all by himself waiting for the signal
Tom Sawyer was to give him at midnight, he
felt so lonesome he wished he was dead :

" The stars was shining and the leaves rustled in
the woods ever so mournful ; and I heard an owl,
away off, who-whooing about somebody that was
dead, and a whippowill and a dog crying about
somebody that was going to die ; and the wind
was trying to whisper something to me, and I
couldn't make out what it was, and so it made the
cold shivers run over me.   Then away out in the
woods I heard that kind of a sound that a ghost
makes when it wants to tell about something that's
on its mind and can't make itself understood, and
so can't rest easy in its grave, and has to go about
that way every night grieving.   I got so down-
hearted and scared I did wish I had some company.   Pretty soon a spider went crawling up my
shoulders, and I flipped it off and it lit in the
candle ; and before I could budge it was all

shrivelled up.   I didn't need anybody to tell me
that that was an awful bad sign and would fetch me
some bad luck, so I was scared and most shook the
clothes off me.   I got up and turned around in my
tracks three times and crossed my breast every
time ; and then I tied up a little lock of my hair
with a thread to keep witches away.   But I hadn't
no confidence.   You do that when you've lost a
horseshoe that you've found, instead of nailing it up
over the door, but I hadn't ever heard anybody say
it was any way to keep off bad luck when you'd
killed a spider."

And, again, later in the story, not at night
this time, but in broad daylight, Huck walks
along a road :

" When I got there it was all still and Sunday-
like, and hot and sunshiny—the hands was gone to
the fields ; and there was them kind of faint
dronings of bugs and flies in the air that makes it
seem so lonesome like everybody's dead and gone ;
and if a breeze fans along and quivers the leaves, it
makes you feel mournful, because you feel like it's
spirits whispering—spirits that's been dead ever so
many years—and you always think they're talking
about *you*.   As a general thing it makes a body
wish *he* was dead, too, and done with it all."

Now, no one of these sentiments is appropriate to Tom Sawyer, who had none of the
feeling for nature which Huck Finn had caught
during his numberless days and nights in the
open air.   Nor could Tom Sawyer either

have seen or set down this instantaneous photograph of a summer storm :

"It would get so dark that it looked all blue-black outside, and lovely; and the rain would thrash along by so thick that the trees off a little ways looked dim and spider-webby; and here would come a blast of wind that would bend the trees down and turn up the pale underside of the leaves; and then a perfect ripper of a gust would follow along and set the branches to tossing their arms as if they was just wild; and next, when it was just about the bluest and blackest—fst! it was as bright as glory, and you'd have a little glimpse of tree-tops a-plunging about, away off yonder in the storm, hundreds of yards further than you could see before; dark as sin again in a second, and now you'd hear the thunder let go with an awful crash, and then go rumbling, grumbling, tumbling down the sky towards the under side of the world, like rolling empty barrels down-stairs, where it's long stairs and they bounce a good deal, you know."

The romantic side of Tom Sawyer is shown in most delightfully humorous fashion in the account of his difficult devices to aid in the easy escape of Jim, the runaway negro. Jim is an admirably drawn character. There have been not a few fine and firm portraits of negroes in recent American fiction, of which Mr. Cable's Bras-Coupé in the "Grandissimes" is perhaps the most vigorous, and Mr. Harris's Mingo and Uncle Remus and Blue Dave are the most gentle. Jim is worthy to rank with

these ; and the essential simplicity and kindliness and generosity of the Southern negro
have never been better shown than here by
Mark Twain.   Nor are Tom Sawyer and
Huck Finn and Jim the only fresh and original figures in Mr. Clemens's book ; on the
contrary, there is scarcely a character of the
many introduced who does not impress the
reader at once as true to life—and therefore
as new, for life is so varied that a portrait
from life is sure to be as good as new.   That
Mr. Clemens draws from life, and yet lifts his
work from the domain of the photograph to
the region of art, is evident to any one who
will give his writing the honest attention which
it deserves.   The chief players in " Huckleberry Finn " are taken from life, no doubt,
but they are so aptly chosen and so broadly
drawn that they are quite as typical as they
are actual.   They have one great charm, all
of them—they are not written about and
about ; they are not described and dissected
and analyzed ; they appear and play their
parts and disappear ; and they leave a sharp
impression of indubitable vitality and individuality.

1886.

II. M. FRANÇOIS COPPÉE'S PROSE TALES.

LIKE Molière, like Boileau, like Regnard, like Voltaire, and like Musset, M. François Coppée was born in Paris, and more than any other of the half-dozen is he a true child of the fair city by the Seine, loving her more ardently, and leaving her less willingly. The facts of his simple and uneventful career have been set forth by his friend M. de Lescure in "François Coppée; l'Homme, la vie et l'Œuvre" (1842-1889). From this we learn that the poet was born in 1842, that he was the youngest child of a poor clerk in the War Department, that he had three elder sisters, one of whom survives still to take care of her brother, that he spent most of his struggling childhood in old houses on the left (and more literary) bank of the Seine, that he was not an apt scholar in his youth, that he began to write verses very early in his teens, and that at last his father died, and he succeeded to the modest position in the War Department, becoming the head of the family

O

at twenty-one. In time he made acquaintance with other young poets, and was admitted into the "Parnassiens," as they were called, followers of Victor Hugo, of Théophile Gautier, of Théodore de Banville, students of new and old rhythms, and seekers after rich rhymes, as ardent in the search as the Argonauts of '49. M. Coppée burnt every one of his juvenile poems, and wrote many another of more cunning workmanship; and of these newer poems two volumes were published in the next few years—"Le Réliquaire" and "Les Intimités"—but they did not sell two hundred copies all told.

Then, in 1869, came the first golden gleam of fortune. "Le Passant," a little one-act comedy in verse, was acted one night at the Odéon, and the next day the name of François Coppée was no longer unknown to any of those who care for letters. "Le Passant" is undeniably artificial, and at bottom it is probably forced in feeling, if not false; but beyond all question the poet believed in it and accepted its truth, and delighted in his work. The sentiment is charmingly youthful, with a spring-like freshness, and the versification is absolutely impeccable. For years M. Coppée was called "the author of 'Le Passant,'" until he came almost to hate his first-born. But only one of his later plays has rivalled it in popular acceptance; this is the pathetic

'Luthier de Crémone," of which there are several adaptations in English. A third one-act play, "Le Pater," forbidden in Paris by the stage censors, was, strangely enough, brought out at Daly's Theatre in New York shortly after as "The Prayer." As a dramatist, M. Coppée continues the romanticist tradition, now a little outworn ; and his longer plays lack the directness of his later poems and prose tales. No one of them has had more than a merely honourable success, and no one has yet shown itself strong enough to stand the perils of translation.

During the dark days of 1870 and 1871 M. Coppée did his duty in the ranks like many another artist in letters and with the brush. Of course he wrote war poems, both during the fighting and after, neither better nor worse, most of them, than the war poems of other French poets. Better than any of these martial rhymes are the "Grève des Forgerons," written just before the war, and "Les Humbles," a volume of verse written shortly after peace had been restored. The "Grève des Forgerons" is a dramatic monologue, in which a striking iron-worker explains how it came to pass that he killed a man, and why he did the deed. It suggests Browning in its mingling of movement and introspection, but it is neither as rugged in form nor as swift in action as the English poet would have made it.

It is in "Les Humbles" that there was first revealed the French poet with whom we of Anglo-Saxon stock can perhaps feel ourselves most in sympathy. The note which dominates the poems in that collection, and in most of M. Coppée's later volumes of verse, is less seldom found in English literature than in French. This is the note of sympathy with the lowly, with the unsuspected victims of fate. It is the note of compassion for those who struggle secretly and in vain, for those who are borne down beneath the burdens of commonplace existence, for those who have never had a chance in life. It is the note we mark now and again, for instance, in the deeper poems of Mr. Austin Dobson. Many of the foremost French authors of late years are mere mandarins, writing exclusively for their peers ; they are Brahmins, despising all outside their own high caste ; they are wholly without bowels of compassion for their fellow-man. Compare, for example, again, the contemptuous and contemning attitude of Flaubert toward the creatures of his own making, whom he regards distantly, as though they were doubtful insects under a microscope, and the warmer tolerance George Eliot shows even for her least worthy characters.

M. Coppée is as detached from his humble heroes and heroines as any one could wish ; he is too profoundly an artist ever to intervene

in his own person ; but he is not chill and
inaccessible in his telling of their little lives
made up of a thousand banalities and lit by a
single gleam of poetry, not cast by the glare
of any great self-sacrifice, but falling from the
pure flame of daily duties performed without
thought of self. " Les Humbles " is but a
gallery of pictures in the manner of the little
masters of Holland,—a series of portraits of
the down-trodden in their every-day garb,
with that suggestion of their inner life which
illuminates every painting by an artist of true
insight. In the old-fashioned sense of the
word there is little "heroic" in " Les Humbles ;"
and there is absolutely nothing of the exag-
gerated larger-than-life-and-twice-as-natural
manner of Victor Hugo, set off with violent
contrasts and startling antitheses. Instead
we have a scholarly poet telling us of the
simple lives of the poor in the simple speech
of the people. M. Coppée has a homeliness
of phrase not unlike that of Theocritus, but
perhaps less consciously literary.

Indeed, nothing more clearly shows the
delicacy of his art than his extraordinary skill
in concealing all trace of artifice, so that a
most carefully constructed poem is seemingly
spontaneous. To most of us French poetry
is rarely interesting ; it is obviously artificial ;
it strikes us as somewhat remote ; possibly
from the enforced use of words of Romance

origin (which, therefore, seem to us secondary)
to describe heart-felt emotion, expressed by
us in words of Teutonic stock (which are
therefore to us primary). Lowell has told
us that it is only the high polish of French
verse that keeps out decay. We do not feel
this in reading the best of M. Coppée's poetry ;
it seems to us as natural an outgrowth almost
as Heine's or Longfellow's. It another essay
Lowell says that perhaps the great charm of
Gray's "Elegy" is to be found "in its embody-
ing that pensively stingless pessimism which
comes with the first gray hair, that vague
sympathy with ourselves which is so much
cheaper than sympathy with others, that placid
melancholy which satisfies the general appe-
tite for an emotion that titillates rather than
wounds." That M. Coppée has put into
French verse, unmusical as it is, qualities
which Lowell finds in Gray's "Elegy" is
evidence that neither in manner nor in matter
is he like most French poets.

But this acceptability of his poetry to ears
attuned to more Teutonic rhythms has not
been won by any accidental dereliction from
the strictest rule of the Parnassians. M. Coppée
has besieged and captured the final fastnesses
of French metrical art, and his work is com-
pletely satisfactory even to de Banville, who
bestrode his hobby of "rich" rhymes as though
it were Pegasus itself. M. Coppée early gave

proof of remarkable skill at the difficult game of French versification, and he still plays it scientifically, and with great good luck. Of late years he has been called upon frequently to sing to order, to write verses for a celebration, and he has always been as ready as Dr. Holmes was once to lay a garland of rhymes on the grave of a hero. The art of writing occasional verse which shall be worthy of the occasion is not a common gift. M. Coppée possesses it abundantly, and his many poems for feasts or fasts are always appropriate, adequate, and dignified.

"Olivier" is M. Coppée's most ambitious longer poem. But it is not in his longer poems that he is seen at his best. What he does to perfection is the *conte en vers*—the tale in verse. The *conte* is a form of fiction in which the French have always delighted, and in which they have always excelled, from the days of the *jongleurs* and the *trouvères*, past the periods of La Fontaine and Voltaire, down to the present. The *conte* is a tale something more than a sketch, it may be, and something less than a short story. In verse it is at times but a mere rhymed anecdote, or it may attain almost to the direct swiftness of a ballad. The "Canterbury Tales" are *contes* most of them, if not all, and so are some of the "Tales of a Wayside Inn." The free and easy tales of Prior were written in imitation of the French

conte en vers, and that likewise was the model
of more than one of the lively narrative poems
of Mr. Austin Dobson.

No one has succeeded more admirably in
the *conte en vers* than M. Coppée. Where
was there ever anything better of its kind than
" L'Enfant de la Balle " ?—that gentle portrait
of the infant phenomenon, framed in a chain
of occasional gibes at the sordid ways of
theatrical managers, and at their hostility
toward poetic plays.   Where is there anything
of a more simple pathos than " L'Épave " ?—
that story of a sailor's son whom the widowed
mother vainly strives to keep from the cruel
waves that killed his father. (It is worthy of
a parenthesis that although the ship M. Coppée
loves best is that which sails the blue shield
of the city of Paris, he knows the sea also, and
he depicts sailors with affectionate fidelity.)
But whether at the sea-side by chance, or
more often in the streets of the city, the poet
seeks for the subject of his story some incident
of daily occurrence made significant by his
interpretation ; he chooses some character
commonplace enough, but made firmer by
conflict with evil and by victory over self.
Those whom he puts into his poems are still
the humble, the forgotten, the neglected, the unknown ; and it is the feelings and the struggles
of these that he tells us, with no maudlin
sentimentality, and with no dead-set at our

sensibilities. The sub-title Mrs. Stowe gave to "Uncle Tom's Cabin" would serve to cover most of M. Coppée's *contes* either in prose or verse ; they are nearly all pictures of "life among the lowly." But there is no forcing of the note in his painting of poverty and labour ; there is no harsh juxtaposition of the blacks and the whites. The tone is always manly and wholesome.

"La Marchande de Journaux" and the other little masterpieces of story-telling in verse are unfortunately untranslatable, as are all poems but a lyric or two now and then, by a happy accident. A translated poem is a boiled strawberry, as someone once brutally put it. But the tales which M. Coppée has written in prose—a true poet's prose, nervous, vigorous, flexible, and firm—these can be Englished by taking thought and time and pains, without which a translation is always a betrayal. Ten of these tales have been rendered into English by Mr. Learned, and the ten chosen for translation are among the best of the twoscore and more of M. Coppée's *contes en prose*. These ten tales are fairly representative of his range and variety. Compare, for example, the passion in the "Foster-sister"—pure, burning, and fatal—with the Black Forest *naïveté* of the "Wooden Shoes of Little Wolff." Contrast the touching pathos of the "Substitute," poignant in his magnificent self-sacrifice, by

which the man who has conquered his shame-
ful past goes back willingly to the horrible
life he has fled from, that he may save from a
like degradation and from an inevitable moral
decay the one friend he has in the world, all
unworthy as this friend is—contrast this with
the story of the gigantic deeds "My Friend
Meutrier" boasts about unceasingly, not knowing that he has been discovered in his little
round of daily domestic duties, making the
coffee of his good old mother, and taking her
poodle out for a walk.

Among these ten there are tales of all sorts,
from the tragic adventure of "An Accident"
to the pendent portraits of the "Two Clowns,"
cutting in its sarcasm, but not bitter; from
the "Captain's Vices," which suggests at once
George Eliot's "Silas Marner" and Mr. Austin
Dobson's "Tale of Polypheme," to the sombre
reverie of the poet "At the Table," a sudden
and searching light cast on the labour and
misery which underlie the luxury of our complex modern existence.   Like "At the Table,"
the "Dramatic Funeral" is a picture more
than it is a story ; it is a marvellous reproduc-
tion of the factitious emotion of the good-
natured stage-folk, who are prone to overact
even their own griefs and joys. The "Dramatic
Funeral" seems to me always as though it
might be a painting of M. Jean Béraud, that
most Parisian of artists, just as certain stories

of Maupassant's inevitably suggest the bold freedom of M. Forain's sketches in black and white.

An ardent admirer of the author of the stories in "The Odd Number" has protested to me that M. Coppée is not an etcher like Maupassant, but rather a painter in water-colours. And why not? Thus might we call M. Alphonse Daudet an artist in pastels, so adroitly does he suggest the very bloom of colour. No doubt M. Coppée's *contes* have not the sharpness of Maupassant's nor the brilliancy of M. Daudet's. But what of it? They have qualities of their own. They have sympathy, poetry, and a power of suggesting pictures not exceeded, I think, by those of either Maupassant or M. Daudet. M. Coppée's street views in Paris, his interiors, his impressionist sketches of life under the shadow of Notre Dame, are convincingly successful. They are intensely to be enjoyed by those of us who take the same keen delight in the varied phases of life in New York. They are not, to my mind, really rivalled either by those of Maupassant, who was a Norman by birth and a nomad by choice, or by those of M. Daudet, who is a native of Provence, although now for thirty years a resident of Paris. M. Coppée is a Parisian from his youth up, and even in prose he is a poet. Perhaps this is why his pictures of Paris are

unsurpassable in their felicity and in their
verity.

It may be fancy, but I seem to see also a
finer morality in M. Coppée's work than in
Maupassant's, or in M. Daudet's, or in that of
almost any other of the Parisian story-tellers
of to-day. In his tales we breathe a purer
moral atmosphere, more wholesome and more
bracing. It is not that M. Coppée probably
thinks of ethics rather than esthetics ; in this
respect his attitude is undoubtedly that of the
others. There is no sermon in his song, or at
least none for those who will not seek it for
themselves ; there is never a hint of a preach-
ment. But for all that, I have found in his
work a trace of the tonic morality which
inheres in Molière, for example—also a Parisian
by birth—and in Rabelais, too, despite his
disguising grossness. This finer morality
comes possibly from a wider and a deeper
survey of the universe ; and it is as different
as possible from the morality which is exter-
nally applied, and which always punishes the
villain in the fifth act.

It is of good augury for our own letters
that the best French fiction of to-day is getting
itself translated in the United States, and that
the liking for it is growing apace. Fiction is
more consciously an art in France than anywhere else, perhaps partly because the French
are now foremost in nearly all forms of artistic

endeavour.   In the short story especially, in the tale, in the *conte*, their supremacy is incontestable, and their skill is shown and their esthetic instinct exemplified partly in the sense of form, in the constructive method which underlies the best short stories, however trifling these may appear to be, and partly in the rigorous suppression of non-essentials, due in a measure, it may be, to the example of Mérimée.   That is an example we in America may study to advantage, and from the men who are writing fiction in France we may gain much.

1890.

III. M. LUDOVIC HALÉVY'S SHORT
STORIES.

TO most readers of English fiction I
fancy that M. Ludovic Helévy is known
chiefly, if not solely, as the author of that most
charming of modern French novels, "The Abbé
Constantin." Some of these readers may have
disliked this or that novel of M. Zola's because
of its bad moral, and this or that novel of M.
Ohnet's because of its bad taste, and all of them
were delighted to discover in M. Halévy's
interesting and artistic work a story written
by a French gentleman for young ladies. Here
and there a scoffer might sneer at the tale of the
old French priest and the young women from
Canada as innocuous and saccharine; but the
story of the good Abbé Constantin and of his
nephew, and of the girl the nephew loved in
spite of her American millions—this story had
the rare good fortune of pleasing at once the
broad public of indiscriminate readers of fiction
and the narrower circle of real lovers of literature. Artificial the atmosphere of the tale
might be, but it was with an artifice at once

delicate and delicious ; and the tale itself won its way into the hearts of the women of America as it had into the hearts of the women of France.

There is even a legend—although how solid a foundation it may have in fact I do not dare to discuss—there is a legend that the lady-superior of a certain convent near Paris was so fascinated by " The Abbé Constantin," and so thoroughly convinced of the piety of its author, that she ordered all his other works, receiving in due season the lively volumes wherein are recorded the sayings and doings of Monsieur and Madame Cardinal, and of the two lovely daughters of Monsieur and Madame Cardinal. To note that these very amusing studies of certain aspects of life in a modern capital originally appeared in that extraordinary journal " La Vie Parisienne "—now sadly degenerate —is enough to indicate that they are not precisely what the good lady-superior expected to receive. We may not say that " La Famille Cardinal " is one of the books every gentleman's library should be without ; but to appreciate its value requires a far different knowledge of the world and of its wickedness than is needed to understand " The Abbé Constantin."

Yet the picture of the good priest and the portraits of the little Cardinals are the work of the same hand, plainly enough. In both of these books, as in " Criquette " (M. Halévy's

only other novel), as in " A Marriage for Love,"
and the two-score other short stories he has
written during the past thirty years, there are
the same artistic qualities, the same sharpnesss
of vision, the same gentle irony, the same constructive skill, and the same dramatic touch.
It is to be remembered always that the author
of " L'Abbé Constantin " is also the half-author
of " Froufrou " and of " Tricoche et Cacolet," as
well as of the librettos of " La Belle Hélène "
and of " La Grande Duchesse de Gerolstein."

In the two novels, as in the two-score short
stories and sketches—the *contes* and the *nou-
velles* which are now springlike idyls and now
wintry episodes, now sombre etching and now
gaily coloured pastels—in all the works of
the story-teller we see the firm grasp of the
dramatist. The characters speak for themselves ; each reveals himself with the swift
directness of the personages of a play. They
are not talked about and about, for all analysis
has been done by the playwright before he
rings up the curtain in the first paragraph.
And the story unrolls itself, also, as rapidly
as does a comedy. The movement is straightforward. There is the cleverness and the ingenuity of the accomplished dramatist, but the
construction has the simplicity of the highest
skill. The arrangement of incidents is so
artistic that it seems inevitable ; and no one is
ever moved to wonder whether or not the tale

might have been better told in different fashion.

Nephew of the composer of " La Juive "— an opera not now heard as often as it deserves, perhaps—and son of a playwright no one of whose productions now survives, M. Halévy grew up in the theatre. At fourteen he was on the free-list of the Opéra, the Opéra Comique, and the Odéon. After he left school and went into the civil service his one wish was to write plays, and so to be able to afford to resign his post. In the civil service he had an inside view of French politics, which gave him a distaste for the mere game of government without in any way impairing the vigour of his patriotism ; as is proved by certain of the short stories dealing with the war of 1870 and the revolt of the Paris Communists. And while he did his work faithfully, he had spare hours to give to literature. He wrote plays and stories, and they were rejected. The manager of the Odéon declared that one early play of M. Halévy's was exactly suited to the Gymnase, and the manager of the Gymnase protested that it was exactly suited to the Odéon. The editor of a daily journal said that one early tale of M. Halévy's was too brief for a novel, and the editor of a weekly paper said that it was too long for a short story.

In time, of course, his luck turned ; he had plays performed and stories published ; and at

last he met M. Henri Meilhac, and entered
on that collaboration of nearly twenty years'
duration to which we owe "Froufrou" and
"Tricoche et Cacolet," on the one hand, and
on the other the books of Offenbach's most
brilliant operas—"Barbebleue," for example,
and "La Périchole." When this collaboration
terminated, shortly before M. Halévy wrote
"The Abbé Constantin," he gave up writing
for the stage. The training of the playwright
he could not give up, if he would, nor the
intimacy with the manners and customs of the
people who live, move, and have their being
on the far side of the curtain.

Obviously M. Halévy is fond of the actors
and the actresses with whom he spent the years
of his manhood. They appear again and again
in his tales ; and in his treatment of them there
is never anything ungentlemanly, as there was
in M. Jean Richepin's recent volume of theatrical sketches. M. Halévy's liking for the
men and women of the stage is deep ; and
wide is his knowledge of their changing moods.
The young Criquette and the old Karikari and
the aged Dancing-master—he knows them all
thoroughly, and he likes them heartily, and he
sympathizes with them cordially.   Indeed,
nowhere can one find more kindly portraits of
the kindly player-folk than in the writings of
this half author of "Froufrou ;" it is as though
the successful dramatist felt ever grateful to-

wards the partners of his toil, the companions of his struggles. He is not blind to their manifold weaknesses, nor is he the dupe of their easy emotionalism, but he is tolerant of their failings, and towards them, at least, his irony is never mordant.

Irony is one of M. Halévy's chief characteristics, perhaps the chiefest. It is gentle when he deals with the people of the stage—far gentler then than when he is dealing with the people of "society," with fashionable folk, with the aristocracy of wealth. When he is telling us of the young loves of millionaires and of million-heiresses, his touch may seem caressing, but for all its softness the velvet paw has claws none the less. It is amusing to note how often M. Halévy has chosen to tell the tale of love among the very rich. The heroine of "The Abbé Constantin" is immensely wealthy, as we all know, and immensely wealthy are the heroines of "Princesse," of "A Grand Marriage," and of "In the Express." Sometimes the heroes and the heroines are not only immensely wealthy, they are also of the loftiest birth ; such, for instance, are the young couple whose acquaintance we make in "Only a Waltz."

There is no trace or taint of snobbery in M. Halévy's treatment of all this magnificence ; there is none of the vulgarity which marks the pages of "Lothair," for example : there is no

mean admiration of mean things. There is,
on the other hand, no bitterness of scourging
satire. He lets us see that all this luxury is a
little cloying, and perhaps not a little ener-
vating. He suggests (although he takes care
never to say it) that perhaps wealth and
birth are not really the best the world can
offer. The amiable egotism of the hero of " In
the Express," and the not unkindly selfishness
of the heroine of that most Parisian love-story,
are set before us without insistence, it is true,
but with an irony so keen that even he who
runs as he reads may not mistake the author's
real opinion of the characters he has evoked.

To say this is to say that M. Halévy's irony
is delicate and playful. There is no harshness
in his manner and no hatred in his mind. We
do not find in his pages any of the pessimism
which is perhaps the dominant characteristic
of the best French fiction of our time. To
M. Halévy, as to every thinking man, life is
serious, no doubt, but it need not be taken
sadly, or even solemnly. To him life seems
still enjoyable, as it must to most of those who
have a vivid sense of humour. He is not dis-
illusioned utterly, he is not reduced to the
blankness of despair as are so many of the
disciples of Flaubert, who are cast into the
outer darkness, and who hopelessly revolt
against the doom they have brought on themselves.

Indeed, it is Merimée that M. Halévy would
hail as his master, and not Flaubert, whom
most of his fellow French writers of fiction
follow blindly.   Now, while the author of
" Salamnbo " was a romanticist turned sour,
the author of " Carmen " was a sentimentalist
sheathed in irony.   To Gustave Flaubert the
world was hideously ugly, and he wished it
strangely and splendidly beautiful, and he
detested it the more because of his impossible
ideal.   To Prosper Merimée the world was
what it is, to be taken and made the best of,
every man keeping himself carefully guarded.
Like Merimée, M. Halévy is detached, but he
is not disenchanted.   His work is more joyous
than Merimée's, if not so vigorous and compact, and his delight in it is less disguised.
Even in the Cardinal sketches there is nothing
that leaves an acrid after-taste, nothing corro-
ding—as there is not seldom in the stronger
and sterner short stories of Maupassant.

More than Maupassant or Flaubert or
Merimée is M. Halévy a Parisian.   Whether
or not the characters of his tale are dwellers
in the capital, whether or not the scene of his
story is laid in the city by the Seine, the point
of view is always Parisian.   The " Circus
Charger " did his duty in the stately avenues
of a noble country place, and " Blacky " performed his task near a rustic waterfall; but
the men who record their intelligent actions

are Parisians of the strictest sect. Even in the
patriotic pieces called forth by the war of 1870,
in the " Insurgent " and in the " Chinese Am-
bassador," it is the siege of Paris and the
struggle of the Communists which seem to the
author most important. His style even, his
swift and limpid prose—the prose which some-
how corresponds to the best *vers de société* in
its brilliancy and buoyancy—is the style of one
who lives at the centre of things. Cardinal
Newman once said that while Livy and Tacitus
and Terence and Seneca wrote Latin, Cicero
wrote Roman ; so while M. Zola on the one
side, and M. Georges Ohnet on the other, may
write French, M. Halévy writes Parisian.

1893.

IV. CERVANTES, ZOLA, KIPLING
AND CO.

M. ANATOLE FRANCE, one of the most discriminating and inconsequent of essayists, has suggested that criticism at its best is little more than a recital of the adventures of the critic's mind in contact with masterpieces. Perhaps one reason why criticism is so infrequently at its best is that the critic's mind is in contact with masterpieces less often than it might be. It is with the writings of his contemporaries that the critic has to deal for the most part ; and how few of any man's contemporaries are masters? It is only by returning resolutely again and again to the masterpieces of the past that a critic is able to sustain his standard—to prevent his taste from sinking to the level of the average of contemporary writing.

And this return, always its own reward, is not without its own surprises. Either the accepted work is worthy of its high repute— and then there is the pleasure of expounding it afresh to a new generation and of showing

its fitness to modern conditions despite its age
—or else it is unworthy and lacks true dura-
bility—and then there is the sad duty of
explaining how it deserved its fame once, and
why it is now outworn. To one critic it happened one summer to be reading " Don
Quixote " (in Mr. Ormsby's nervous and satisfactory translation), when he received, by the
same post, the " Débâcle " of M. Emile Zola,
and the " Naulahka " of Mr. Rudyard Kipling
and the late Wolcott Balestier ; and when he
had made an end of the perusal of these three
books—the novel of the Spaniard, the novel
of the Frenchman, and the novel of the
Englishman and the American, it occurred to
him that he had in them material for a literary
comparison not without a certain piquancy.
To criticise these three books adequately would
permit the writing of the history of fiction
during the past three centuries ; it would
authorize a thorough discussion of the principles of the novelist's art, as these have been
developed by the many mighty story-tellers
who lived after Cervantes and before M.
Zola.

For a siege as formidable as this I have not
the critical apparatus, even if I had the desire.
The most that I can do here is to set down
honestly and frankly a few of my impressions
as I read in turn these three novels, strangely
consorted and sharply contrasting. To sum

up the merits of M. Zola's book is easy ; and
it is not hard to form and to formulate an
opinion about the Indo-American tale of the
two young collaborators ; but the great work
of Cervantes is not so lightly disposed of.
The danger of any effort to record the adventures of the critic's mind in contact with a
masterpiece like "Don Quixote" is that it is exceedingly difficult for the critic to be frank with
himself or honest with his readers.   His mind
does not come squarely in contact with the
masterpiece ; it is warded off by the cloud of
commentators · with whom every masterpiece
is encompassed about.   He can read only
through the spectacles of the countless critics
who have preceded him.   He knows what he
ought to think about " Don Quixote," and
this makes it almost impossible for him to
think for himself as he ought.

For the critic in search of mental adventures,
it is a safeguard to have a hearty distrust of
philosophic criticism, so-called—to have a profound disbelief in the allegorical interpretation
of simple stories.   Cervantes was like all the
other great makers of fiction in that he wrote
first to amuse himself and to relieve himself
and only secondarily to amuse his readers, to
move them, to instruct them even.

" There is no mighty purpose in this book,"
is a proper motto for the title page of most of
the masterpieces in which philosophical criti-

cism sees a myriad of mighty purposes and which were written easily and carelessly, and with no intention of creating a masterpiece, and with scarcely a thought of the message which the world has since deciphered between the lines. "He builded better than he knew" is true of most great writers ; perhaps it is not wholly true of Dante and of Milton, who were conscious artists always, and careful ; but it is absolutely true of Shakespeare and of Cervantes. In their pages we find many a moral which would surprise them ; and into their words we are forever reading meanings of our own of which they had never a suspicion. That "Hamlet" and "Don Quixote" yield up to us to-day messages and morals their straightforward authors never intended, is perhaps the best possible evidence that "Hamlet" and "Don Quixote" are masterpieces. The work of art which has only the message and the moral its maker intended, is likely to be thin and barren.

The author of "Hamlet" was like his close contemporary, the author of "Don Quixote," in that he thought less apparently of the great work which has survived in the affections of the world for two centuries and a half, than he thought of his other writings, now recalled chiefly because they are due to the pen which gave us also the masterpieces. Obviously, Cervantes did not read the proof of "Don

Quixote," the first editions of which abound in printer's errors, almost as many and as serious as those which mar the first folio of Shakespeare. It would be easy to maintain the assertion that Cervantes set as little store by "Don Quixote" as Shakespeare did by "Hamlet" and its fellows, the great Spaniard esteeming more highly his plays and his poems, just as Shakespeare seems to have cherished rather his poetry than his plays, each man holding lightly that which he had wrought most readily and with least effort.

Indeed the carelessness with which Cervantes has treated his masterpiece is one of the first things to strike a critic who reads the seventeenth century story with nineteenth century fastidiousness. Conscious of the temerity of my opinion, and aware of the awful fate which may befall me for declaring it, I venture to suggest that the art of fiction is a finer art to-day than it was when "Don Quixote" was written. In the whole history of story-telling there is no greater name than the name of Cervantes; but it would be a painful reflection on progress if the efforts of successive generations of novelists—however inferior to him any one of these might be—had not put the art forward. The writers of fiction nowadays are scrupulous where Cervantes was reckless; they take thought where he gave none. Merely in the mechanism of plot, in

the joinery of incident, in the craftsmanship of
story telling, "Don Quixote" is indisputably
less skilful than M. Zola's "Débâcle," or the
Kipling-Balestier "Naulahka"—however inferior these may be in more vital points.

Consider for a moment the awkward pre-
tence of a translation from the manuscript of
the Moor, Hamet Benengeli, as needless as it
is ill-sustained. Consider the frank artlessness
of the narrative with its irrelevant tales in-
jected into the manuscript merely because
Cervantes happened to have them on hand.
Consider the many anachronisms and inconsistencies which Cervantes troubled himself
about quite as little as Shakespeare thought
or cared whether or not Bohemia was a desert
country by the sea. Consider the extraordinary series of coincidencies which brought together at the inn four marvellously beautiful
women, when the captive met his brother and
Cardenio recovered Luscinda, all of which
is improbable to the vanishing point and all
of which, worse yet, has nothing whatever to
do with the true subject of the story. Considering all these slovenlinesses, it is impossible not to wonder whether the art of fiction
did not retrograde with Cervantes, for both
Boccaccio and Chaucer had attained vigour
and suppleness in narrative; their tales were
naif, no doubt, and direct, but they were
always artfully composed and presented. To

this day the "Decameron" and the "Canterbury Tales" are models of simple story telling. Great as are his other qualities, Cervantes, merely as a teller of tales, is as inferior to Boccaccio and to Chaucer, as he is superior to Rabelais.

It is in its humanity, in its presentation of men and women, in its character-drawing, as the modern phrase is, that the story of Cervantes excels all the stories of Boccaccio, of Chaucer and of Rabelais. Alongside the gigantic figure of the Knight of La Mancha, what are the characters in the brilliant little comedies of Chaucer and of Boccaccio but thumb-nail sketches? What are Gargantua and Panurge but broad caricatures, when compared with the delicately limned "Don Quixote?" Where, before, had any one put into fiction so much of our everyday humanity? And what, after all, do we seek in a novel, if it is not human nature? To catch mankind in the act, as it were; to surprise the secrets of character and to show its springs; to get into literature the very trick of life itself; to display the variety of human existence, its richness, its breadth, its intensity; to do these things with unforced humour, with unfailing good-humour, with good-will toward all men, with tolerance, with benignity, with loving-kindness—this is what no writer of fiction had done before Cervantes wrote "Don Quixote," and this is what no writer of fiction

has ever done better than Cervantes did it
when he wrote " Don Quixote."

Chaucer is shrewd and kindly at once, but
even he lacks the commingled benevolence
and worldly wisdom of Cervantes. The
characters of the " Canterbury Tales " have
a sharper outline than the more softly rounded
figures with whom Don Quixote is associated.
Chaucer had a full share of the milk of
human kindness, but there is the very cream
of it in Cervantes. Perhaps there is no better
test of the greatness of a humourist than this
—that his humour has no curdling acidity. It
is easy to amuse when there is a willingness to
wound wantonly ; and Swift, though he may
laugh and shake in Rabelais' easy-chair, does
not fill that huge throne, because he has
the pettiness of brutality. " Gulliver " is inferior to " Gargantua " in that the author
of the former hated humanity, while the
author of the latter loved his fellow-man, and
took life easily and was happy.

Cervantes was not a merry man and he had
a hard life and perhaps he wrote his great book
in prison, but there is no discontent in " Don
Quixote." There is a wholesome philosophy
in it and a willingness to make the best of the
world, a world which is not so bad after
all. " Don Quixote " is a very long book, not
so long as " Amadis of Gaul," or as the
romances of Mademoiselle de Scudéry, or as

the "Three Musketeers" with its tail of
sequels, but longer even than "Daniel De-
ronda" and than "Robert Elsmere;" it is
very long and it is crowded with characters,
but among all these people there is no one
man or woman whom we hate—there is no
one whom the author despises or insults.
Cervantes is not severe with the children of
his brain ; he loves them all ; he treats them
all with the toleration which comes of perfect
understanding. Here, indeed, is the quality
in which he is most modern, in which he
is still unsurpassable. Fielding caught it
from him ; and Thackeray, who borrowed so
many things from Fielding and so much, did
not take over this also, or he could never have
pursued and run down and harried Becky
Sharp as he did.

Just as Fielding began "Joseph Andrews"
merely to guy Richardson's virtuous Pamela,
and just as he ended by falling in love with his
own handiwork and by giving us the exquisite
portrait of Parson Adams, so Cervantes, in-
tending at first little more than to break a
lance with the knights of romance, came to
respect his own work more and more, and to
treat Don Quixote with increasing courtesy.
Much of the first part is horse-play, fun of the
most robust sort. The humour of physical
misadventure is rarely refined, and it takes
a stout stomach to relish some of Don

Quixote's earlier misfortunes. Even in the
Second Part, the practical joke of the belled
cats may fairly be called cruel, and it is altogether unworthy of the hero. Perhaps this is
nineteenth century hypercriticism, but Cervantes is to blame if he has presented to us a
character so lovable that we revolt when anyone takes an unfair advantage of him.

We do not resent the indignities which
befall Sancho, for he has a tough hide and a
stout heart and a mouth full of proverbs for
his own consolation. Yet, in his way, the
worthy squire is as lovable as the honourable
knight he served. Just as Sam Weller (who
made the success of the "Pickwick Papers")
was an afterthought, so was Sancho, who
owed his being apparently to the chance remark of the Landlord, that a knight should
be attended by a squire. Nothing reveals the
genius of Cervantes more plainly than the development of Sancho Panza, who was at first
only a clown, nothing but a droll, a variant of
the gracioso or low comedian accompanying
the hero of every Spanish comedy. By degrees
he is elevated from a mere mask into an
actual man, the mouthpiece of our common
humanity. The lofty Knight of La Mancha,
with his impossible aspirations, may be taken
as a personification of the soul, while Sancho
is the body—of the earth, earthy, and having
his feet on the ground firmly. " There is a

moral in ' Don Quixote,' " said Lowell, " and
a very profound one, whether Cervantes consciously put it there or not, and it is this :
That whoever quarrels with the nature of
things, wittingly or unwittingly, is certain to get
the worst of it." Sancho had never a quarrel
with the nature of things.

Lowell also reminded us that " Cervantes is
the father of the modern novel, in so far as it
has become a study and delineation of character, instead of being a narrative seeking to
interest by situation and incident." " Don
Quixote " is one of the most original of stories ;
it had no predecessors of its kind, and it
evolved itself by the spontaneous generation
of genius. But its posterity is as ample as its
ancestry was meagre. When we see Fielding's
Parson Adams, or Goldsmith's Dr. Primrose,
or Scott's Antiquary, we see children of
Don Quixote. When we follow Mr. Pickwick in his foolish wanderings, when we listen
to Tartarin of Tarascon telling of the lions he
has slain, when we hear Col. Carter of Carters-
ville urging the desire of the Garden Spot of
Virginia for an outlet to the sea, we have
before us the progeny of the Knight of the
Sorrowful Countenance. The make-believe of
Tom Sawyer in trying to get Jim out of
prison in full accordance with the authorities,
recalls Don Quixote's going mad in imitation
of Orlando ; and in the pages of an earlier

Q

American humorist than Mark Twain, in
Irving's "Knickerbocker," there is more than
a hint of the manner of Cervantes. As Lowell
puts it sharply, "the pedigrees of books are
as interesting and instructive as those of
men."

If Cervantes was the father of the modern
novel, we may wonder what he would think
of some of his great-great-grandchildren.
What, for example, would be his opinion
of the "Naulahka," written by a Londoner
who has been East and by a New Yorker who
had been West? Cervantes grew to manhood
with the sons of the Conquistadores, with the
men of iron who had won for Spain the golden
lands of Mexico and Peru; would he have
foregathered with the Argonauts of Forty-
Nine? A scant half-century before his birth
the Portuguese had pushed their way around
Africa in search of Golconda and Cathay;
would he have been interested by this story
of the West and the East?

Of one thing, indeed, we may fairly be certain—that Cervantes would not have been at
all surprised by the manner of the "Naulahka,"
for it is a tale of a kind he was abundantly
familiar with. It is a story of a sort older by
far than "Don Quixote;" it is a story, in fact,
of the sort that "Don Quixote" was written
to satirize. In the new tale we have new
dresses, of course, and new scenery and new

properties, but the tale itself is the old, old story of the hero in search of adventures ; it is the tale of the hero always on the brink of death, but bearing a charmed life ; it is the tale of the hero skilled in all manner of sports, expert with all manner of weapons, fertile in resource and prompt in decision ; it is the tale, in short, of the bravura hero of concert-pitch romance. What is Tarvin of Topaz but Amadis of Gaul ? What is the Crichton of Colorado but Palmerin of England, with all the modern improvements ? What is he but Belianis of Greece, brought down to date ?

The death-dealing and unkillable Tarvin may also be called a Yankee d'Artagnan. Like the Gascon hero, he goes in search of jewels of great price ; but he is a nobler hero even than Dumas's, for he is alone, while the three musketeers were always four. Tarvin, indeed, is the very acme of heroes, than which there can be no man more accomplished and versatile—not even Mr. Barnes of New York, or Mr. Potter of Texas. He is a real-estate boomer and an engineer ; he has been a broncho-breaker and a telegraph operator ; he is a dead-shot with a revolver, hitting a half-dollar spun in the air while keeping an easy seat on a bucking horse.

The main adventure in which the heroic Tarvin is engaged is simply childish ; the word need not be taken as a reproach—I merely mean that it is a thing to be told to amuse children. It is what the French call a *conte à dormir debout.* Like most of the romantic fiction of this late day, the " Naulahka " reveals rather invention than imagination. It is ingeniously constructed ; it has not a little of the cleverness its authors have shown in other work ; it has passages of beauty ; it gives the reader moments of excitement ; it is lighted now and again by flashes of insight ; and, as a whole, it is a hollow disappointment.

And the reason is not far to seek. It is because romance of this sort is not what either of the collaborators did best. It is because neither Mr. Kipling nor his brother-in-law could put his whole strength into so hopeless a make - believe. Balestier was a realist ; beyond all question, the man who wrote the little tale of " Reffey " was a realist, with the imagination a true realist needs more than the ordinary romanticist. Mr. Kipling is sometimes a realist and sometimes an idealist ; he is a humorist often, and, when he is at his best, he is a poet also. Why did two such men join forces in a vain effort to pump the breath of life into a disestablished idol ?

Of course the " Naulahka " is not without touches of character worthy of the author of " The Courting of Dinah Shadd," although

there is little or nothing in it really worthy of
the author of " The Gate of a Hundred Sor-
rows " and of " Without Benefit of Clergy."
The gipsy queen is a fine conception, and her
son is a live child, and the heir-apparent is
also a human being ; all of these ring true.
And here and there in the Indian chapters of
the story are other evidences of Mr. Kipling's
robust talent, of his knack of the unhackneyed
epithet, of his power of revealing character as
by a lightning flash.   Perhaps it is due to the
milder influence of his collaborator that there
is in the " Naulahka " less of the bluster, of the
swagger, of the precocious knowingness which
made some of the " Plain Tales from the
Hills " offensive in the eyes of those who do
not like a style made up wholly of the primary
colours.   There is less also of the violence
which was the key-note of the " Light that
Failed ; " and Mr. Kipling is no longer looking
for effects, immediate, obvious and barbaric,—
like the architecture of the India his stories
give us so strong a desire not to visit.

While the " Naulahka " is, as I have said,
the kind of a story which was popular a full
century before " Don Quixote " was written,
" La Débâcle " is the kind of a story which
has come into fashion two and a half centuries
after " Don Quixote " first appeared.   If Cervantes would find himself at home in reading
the adventures of Tarvin of Topaz, what

would he think of M. Zola's solidly built and
broadly painted panorama of the Second
Empire's catastrophe ? Perhaps, as an old
soldier, as one who had fought at Lepanto,
Cervantes would be most impressed by the
sustained force of M. Zola's battle-pieces, than
which there are none more vigorous in all
fiction. Not Stendahl's Waterloo, not Victor
Hugo's, not Thackeray's—done by indirection,
but all the more moving for that—not Tolstoi's
Sevastopol even, gives the reader so vivid a
realization of the waste of war, of its destruc-
tiveness, of the weariness of it and the hunger,
of the horrors of every kind which are inevitable and necessary, and which M. Zola makes
us feel more keenly than Callot could or
Verestchagin.

There is in "La Débâcle" little of the
realism M. Zola has praised, little or nothing
of the naturalism he has proclaimed ; there is
an epic simplicity, a mighty movement, a
cyclopean architecture, not to be found in the
work of any other novelist in all the luminous
list of names since Cervantes. We have here
no miniature portraits of dandy soldiers ; we
have no mere genre painting of troops in
picturesque attitudes ; we have rather a series
of masterly frescoes, brushed in boldly with a
broad sweep of the arm, without hesitancy,
with the consciousness of strength. M. Zola
has M. Taine's faculty of accumulating typical

details ; he has the same power of handling immense masses of facts and of compelling each into its proper place ; and never has he used this faculty and this power to better advantage than in " La Débâcle "—not even in " Germinal."

The story is far too long ; it has two hundred pages too many ; it is extended to include the last wild struggle of the Commune ; it grows wearisome at last ; but what a splendid succession of pictures is presented to us before we feel the first fatigue ! We are made to see the incredible mismanagement of the imperial army, due to mingled knavery and incompetence ; we are shown the complete collapse of the French commissariat and ordnance department ; we are made spectators of the moral disintegration of impending defeat as the French were shut in by the inexorable iron ring of the Germans ; we have brought before us the whole helpless empire, from the invalid monarch down to the privates and the peasants.

The unending passage of the Prussian artillery through the village by night at a hard gallop ; the sudden vision, in the midst of the battle, of a peasant ploughing peacefully, in a hidden hollow—repeated again when the fight is over ; the execution of Weiss under the eyes of his wife, after a defence of his house, which is a realization in words of " The Last Cartridge ; " the ghastly group of the dead

Zouaves carousing ; the frantic charge of the
riderless horses across the silent battlefield ;
the assassination of Goliath in the presence of
his child ; these are things which cling to the
memory obstinately. These are scenes also
which Cervantes would appreciate as he would
appreciate the massive structure of "La Débâcle" when compared with the haphazard
incidents and the hesitating plot of "Don
Quixote."

What Cervantes would most miss in M. Zola's
book would be joyousness and humour. M.
Zola has no humour, either positive or negative
—positive which breaks in upon the serious-
ness of the reader, or negative which prevents
the author from taking himself too seriously.
M. Zola has little joy in life, although he has
softened of late. Once he saw all mankind
darkly, as though he hated humanity or de-
spised it ; and the characters in his novels
were etched by the acid of his malice. Now
he uses a gentler crayon and he sketches with
suaver outlines ; he is not unfair even towards
the Germans. There are in "La Débâcle"
men and women we can like ;—although there
is no one to love as we love Don Quixote and
Sancho. Brutal is what M. Zola used to be,
brutal and dirty. He is not brutal now and
he is less dirty. He is still fond of foul words
and there are half-a-dozen of them repeated
again and again in "La Débâcle." But as a

whole, the story is surprisingly clean. There is nothing in it to shock Cervantes certainly, for he too could be plain-spoken at times,— quite as plain-spoken as M. Zola. But whatever his speech, however frank and hearty, however exactly he reproduces the vocabulary of the common people, the mind of Cervantes was always clean, pure, lofty.

1892.

V. MR. CHARLES DUDLEY WARNER AS
A WRITER OF FICTION.

THE late Matthew Arnold had an infi-
nitely wider outlook than any of his
contemporaries among British critics, but none
the less was he capable of insularity on occasion, as when he made his taunting remark
about the people of the United States reading
the works of "a native author named Roe"
rather than the masterpieces of literature;—
the remark being made at the very moment
when the people of Great Britain were reading
the works of a native author named Haggard,
when the people of France were reading the
works of a native author named Ohnet, and
when the people of Germany were reading
the works of a native author named "Marlitt."
And yet a few years before the distinguished
critic sneered thus unsuccessfully at this tran-
sient failing of ours, which happened to have
at the time an equivalent in every other
country, there was another American weakness at which he could have girded more
effectively. This weakness was an uneasy

desire for a strange and portentous work of
fiction which was to be hailed at once, on its
appearance, as The Great American Novel.
The satirist would have had a fair target in
this parochial expectancy of the impossible.
How should there ever be so monstrous an
entity as The Great American Novel? Is
there such a thing as The Great British
Novel, or The Great French Novel? And
if there is, what is the name thereof, and who
proclaimed and proved its unique greatness?

It is pleasant to observe that this silly
demand for an impossible object, frequent
enough when we had no novelists, or very
few, has died away now that we have a compact corps of trained writers of fiction—a
corps in which promising recruits are enlisted
almost every month. These conscripts in
story-telling are often veterans in other divi-
sions of the literary body; and they are
drawn especially from the rapidly thinning
ranks of the essayists. It may be doubted
whether the historians of literature have
hitherto paid sufficient attention to the strong
influence of the English essayists upon the
development of the English novel. Addison
and Steele made the way straight for Henry
Fielding and for Jane Austen. " Rasselas "
and the " Vicar of Wakefield " are simply
numbers of the " Rambler " and of the " Citizen
of the World " somewhat expanded. So

Mr. Howells, after " Suburban Sketches," set out on " Their Wedding Journey" and formed " A Chance Acquaintance "; so Mr. Charles Dudley Warner, after spending a "Summer in a Garden" and after making a series of "Back-Log Studies," went away also on " Their Pilgrimage" and took part in " A Little Journey in the World."

It was Tom Moore who pointed out in his memoir of Sheridan that English comedy had been the work of very young men—which would tend to account for its vivacity, perhaps, and for its immaturity also. That the novelists of our language have, on the contrary, flowered later in life, more often than not, has also been noted before now. Richardson was fifty when he celebrated the triumph of virtue in " Pamela "; Fielding was thirty-five when he made fun of poor Pamela by giving her a brother, " Joseph Andrews "; Scott was forty when he finally finished " Waverley "; Thackeray did not begin " Vanity Fair," and George Eliot did not sketch the first of her " Scenes of Clerical Life," until they had reached one-half of the allotted limit of threescore years and ten ; and Mr. Howells was about the same age when he took his first timid flight in fiction with " Their Wedding Journey." Mr. Warner was older than Richardson when he turned story-teller and wrote the fascinating journal

of " Their Pilgrimage," and he was full sixty
when he followed this travel tale with a full-
fledged novel, " A Little Journey in the
World." Like Fielding and Scott, like Thackeray and Mr. Howells, Mr. Warner had made
proof of his literary faculty long before he
ventured into the doubtful labyrinth of fiction,
wherein the most accomplished man of letters
may lose his way if he cannot keep a firm
grasp of the thread of interest, the only clue
which can guide him and his readers to a
joyful safety.

It is characteristic of Mr. Warner's modesty
that even now, when he has come to his reward, when he has made a hit as a humorist,
when he has been welcomed as a writer of
travels, when he has won a place for himself
in the front rank of essayists, when he has
appeared twice as a novelist, that he is wont
to speak of himself not as a man of letters,
but as a journalist. His career has the unexpectedness to be discovered in the lives of so
many energetic Americans who set out in one
direction and then go suddenly in another—
reaching their original goal in the end, it may
be, but only after a circumnavigation of the
globe. Born in Massachusetts in 1829, gra-
duating from Hamilton in 1851, he lived on
the frontier for a year or two, and then studied
law at the University of Pennsylvania.
He practised as a lawyer in Chicago until

1860, when he went to Hartford to take
charge of a paper since consolidated with the
"Courant" (in which Mr. Warner is still
interested). His editorial writing was so fresh
and vigorous that his articles were not only
copied with the usual credit, but stolen also
without compunction ; one New Jersey newspaper man even formed the habit of daily
transferring to his own editorial columns the
article Mr. Warner had published the day
before in the Hartford "Courant."

It was in the spring of 1870 that Mr. Warner
began to contribute to the "Courant " a series of
papers chronicling the experiences and the mis-
adventures of an amateur gardener. Amusing
as these little essays were, they had none of
the "acrobatic comedy" (as it has been called)
of the ordinary newspaper funny man, who
has his easily learnt formulas for extracting
laughs. The humour of Mr. Warner's record
of his tribulations in the garden was not
machine-made ; it was original, individual,
delicate, playful, and at bottom thoughtful ;
it was the easy fooling of a gentleman and a
scholar. It happened to hit the popular taste,
and the successive papers were copied far and
wide, and quoted and talked about, and finally
gathered into a book. "My Summer in a
Garden" was popular not only in the United
States but in Great Britain as well, where,
indeed, three rival publishers showed their

appreciation by reprinting it promptly.   One
of these gentry even changed the title and
chose to call the little book " Pusley"; but
no one of the three thought it needful to
transmit any pecuniary honorarium to the
American author; although it was even then
possible to make transfers of money by the
Atlantic cable.

After the success of " My Summer in a
Garden," the author wrote a series of
" Back-Log Studies," suggested possibly by
the " Autocrat of the Breakfast Table," and
possibly by the " Reveries of a Bachelor," and
possibly owing nothing to either of these, for
it was full of what we now know to be the
flavour of Mr. Warner's own personality.   The
first requisite of an essayist, the one thing
needful, without which he is as nothing, is to
have his own point of view, to own himself, to
be his own master.   The artist, so Goethe
tells us, " make what contortions he will, can
bring to light only his own individuality";
Mr. Warner is no literary contortionist, and
it is without violence or wrench that he brings
his individuality to light.   The more amusing
side of this individuality had been shown in
" My Summer in a Garden," and it was rather
the deeper aspect which was first revealed in
" Back-Log Studies," wherein the wit and the
humour flame up and crackle and sparkle, while
the thought beneath glows and burns steadily.

Probably Mr. Warner himself would not approve of any suggestion that all his various
writings, editorial articles, essays, books of
travels, biographies, social studies — or at
least such of them as had appeared before
1886 — were merely preparations for their
author's first venture into fiction.   But
certainly, and whatever their value may
be in other respects, they were each in its
different degree advantageous to him when he
took up the new art of story-telling.   In
writing them Mr. Warner had trained his eye
and his hand ; he had proved his weapons,
and he had measured himself.   The change of
the essayist into the novelist was a slow development, and not a sudden expansion, as
had been the change of the lawyer into the
journalist a quarter of a century before.   He
could not but be aware that he had the literary
faculty in a high degree; it remained to be seen
whether he had also the gift of story-telling,
without which the novelist is as naught.

It does not seem to me that this crucial
question is answered in " Their Pilgrimage."
In this first attempt Mr. Warner was diffident
and modest.   While there is more incident in
" Their Pilgrimage " than there was in Curtis's
first attempt at fiction, " The Potiphar Papers,"
and more even than there is in Mr. Howell's
" Their Wedding Journey," still the book is
hardly to be classed among novels, unless, in-

deed, there were a separate division for topo-
graphic fiction. It is the record of a voyage
of discovery among the American summer re-
sorts, extending from Bar Harbour to the
White Sulphur, and including Saratoga and
Long Branch, Newport and Narragansett Pier
and Niagara. It was natural that the essayist
turning novelist should be a portrayer of social
conditions rather than a story-teller, pure and
simple. He has a story to tell, of course (he
is no needy knife-grinder), and he tells it well,
bringing the hero to the proposal promptly,
and allowing the heroine the cherished privilege of self-sacrifice; but none the less are
we allowed to guess that the shifting panorama is almost as interesting as are the figures
making love in the foreground. Now and
again, as is the duty of the essayist, he lets us
catch a glimpse of his own individuality, not
suppressing it vigorously, as is the wont of the
most advanced story-tellers of to-day.

But still, the book "lets itself be read," to
use the useful German phrase. However slight
as a story, it is delightful as the work of an
accomplished man of letters, deftly sketching
a bit of scenery here and adroitly outlining a
bit of character there. And especially does it
abound in good talk—in good talk which is
not merely a sequence of clever phrases, but
really *talk*, with the flavour of give and take,
to and fro, hit or miss, cut and thrust, which

R

is the essence of friendly conversation. The
late Lord Houghton declared that " good conversation is to ordinary talk what whist is to
playing cards ; " and Mr. Warner has here
proved himself a most expert whist-player,
with the fullest understanding of American
leads. " A man always talks badly who has
nothing to say," Voltaire remarked ; but it
does not follow that the reverse is true, and
that the man who has something to say is
sure to talk well. Mr. Warner and Mr. Warner's companions in " Their Pilgrimage " have
always something to say, and something to
which the reader is delighted to listen ; and
they say it in such fashion as to make conversation seem the very cream of culture.

In " Their Pilgrimage " Mr. Warner showed
that he had a firm grasp of the essential facts
of American life and character ; in " A Little
Journey in the World " he revealed that he had
also mastered the art of fiction, and was able
to fix the reader's attention not on the scenery
and the chorus which had amused us in the
earlier book, but on the characters of the men
and women, and on the influence of these
characters one on the other. He had turned
from the externals of existence to the internals.
He had thrust the panorama into the background and concentrated his attention on the
figures in the foreground. And these figures
are well worthy of his attention and of ours.

He groups together the delicate, sensitive New England girl of high ideals and the rather common but clever New York girl—of a kind seen in the city often enough, and yet not at all a typical New York girl, if such an entity may be said to exist. He shows us a new variety of the English lord whom it is the duty of the American girl to reject; and he makes us see what a fine fellow the Englishman is, and what a mistake the girl makes in accepting, instead of his, the love of a Wall Street speculator, handsome, bold, scheming, and unscrupulous. And here it is that Mr. Warner proves at once his insight into life and his newly-acquired skill as a story-teller; he makes us see and understand, and even accept as inevitable, the slow process of deterioration which follows on the mating of a young woman of lofty standards with a dominating character of coarser and tougher substance. The disintegration of Margaret's moral fibre under the repeated shocks of worldliness, incessantly recurring, until at last the strain breaks down all resistance, seems to me one of the finest things in recent American literature.

At the end of " A Little Journey in the World," the gentle Margaret, after wedding the daring speculator Henderson, finally faded away and died, whereupon the swift vengeance of Heaven pursued Henderson, and the book closes with his marriage to the easy-going

Carmen. That these two characters, thus fitly disposed of, should reappear in " The Golden House " is a surprise, not to say a shock, and yet it must be confessed that the result justifies Mr. Warner's daring. We can see now that the author was right in thinking that the career of Henderson, and also the career of his second wife, might be carried further with advantage. Henderson's career, indeed, the author has seen fit to carry out to the end—to his sudden and lonely death in the midst of his millions.

Of all the many attempts to represent in fiction the American money-maker, the man who has amassed an immense fortune, and who goes on increasing it with no thought of resting from his labour, the man who exists solely for the sake of making money, sur-rendering all tastes that interfere with this passion, giving up everything else, abandon-ing his whole life to gain, and not from any sordid avarice, not even from any great desire to use what he accumulates, but moved mainly by an interest in the sport of speculation, and finding the zest of his life in the game of money-making, wholly regardless of the cash value of the stakes—of all the many efforts to put such a man before us in the pages of a novel, this study of Mr. Warner's seems to me to be the most successful. Henderson is vigorously presented, and we get to know

him, and to understand how it is that he is
not unkindly, and that he is absolutely unscrupulous. We perceive why he has no
malice toward those he injured by his scheming, while he bears them no ill-will even after
he has ruined them. We see how all the
better impulses of the man have been starved
and choked by the growth of the one all-
absorbing passion ; and it is not without pity
that we discover that not only his impulses,
but his tastes, his minor interests in life, his
faculty of enjoyment, have been eliminated,
one by one, until at last he has nothing left
but the one thing which he has set his heart
on, and to which he has bent his whole being.
Then at length even this one thing loses its
savour, and is as dust and ashes in his mouth.
At the very acme and climax of his triumph
Henderson knows that his life has been a
failure.

This boldly projected figure of Henderson
dominates the book as his exemplars tower
aloft over the social organization of our time.
In our modern society the millionaire has in
great measure taken the place held aforetime
by the nobleman ; and it may very well be
that we allow him to enjoy too many of the
feudal advantages of his predecessor. Perhaps Mr. Kidd is right in thinking that we
are according to captains of industry an
undue proportion of the powers and of the

honours which were formerly bestowed rightly
enough on commanders in war.   One of the
merits of " The Golden House " is that it forces
the reader to take thought about society.
The book is no tract, no parable, no allegory,
no *Tendenz-Roman* even, as the Germans
phrase it, no novel with a purpose ; it is a
story, pure and simple, with strongly drawn
characters, in whose sayings and doings we
are interested for their own sakes ; but none
the less even the casual reader who turns its
pages carelessly has forced upon him a consciousness that our social system is strangely
inadequate and startlingly imperfect.

Perhaps nothing is more harmful to-day
than the frequent denunciations of the existing order of things with the obvious inference
that a society so deformed needs to be rooted
up and cleared away and made over.   What
ought to be plain to us is that, with all the
defects of the social organization in our time,
this organization is less defective than it
ever was before ; that there has been steady
progress in the world from generation to
generation ; that there has been no century
in which the average man has not been
better off than he was in the previous century ; that it is our duty to do all that in
us lies to help forward this progress ; and that
nothing tends to retard this improvement
more than violent and inflammatory declama-

tion.   The pessimist who refuses to believe in
any advance is quite as wrong as the optimist
who denies that there is any necessity for a
forward movement.   Now, as always, discontent is a duty, for it is a condition precedent to progress.   It is not discontent that
throws the dynamite bomb ; it is despair.

While Mr. Warner's novel is the work of a
thinker, and while it affords food for thought
even to the cursory reader, it is wholly free
from denunciation.   By its perusal we are led
not to wish to destroy society, but rather to
desire its reorganization ; and we are made at
least to suspect the complexity of the problem.
Mr. Warner shows us the poor as well as the
rich—Mulberry Bend after Madison Avenue
—and he does not idealize the one more than
the other.   Perhaps, after all, the pinch of
poverty does not squeeze the soul more than
the weight of riches—although it numbs the
body sooner.

It is poverty that saves Jack Delancy, who
is perhaps to be called the hero of " The
Golden House," and who is certainly a most
skilful piece of portraiture.   We all know
Jack ; he is the clever young fellow, moving
easily through life along the line of least resistance, and having no shadows in his path
except when he stands in his own light.   If
such a young man has had the good fortune
to be born poor, he can save himself, and the

world is the richer by a fine fellow.   If he has
the bad luck of Jack Delancy, and inherits
twenty thousand dollars a year, he is not
likely to save himself, for ennui is the devil's
advocate—and as Mr. Warner tersely puts it,
"wherever the devil is, there is always a
quorum present for business."   Even after
Jack marries an ideal wife his fate is in doubt,
and it needs not only her aid but the sharp
douche of sudden poverty to stimulate him
into making the best of his life.

As it is no fairy tale that Mr. Warner is
writing, he does not let Jack reform in the
twinkling of an eye, but only after a long
struggle with himself and his habits ; for
while a noble impulse may make a man
volunteer for a forlorn hope, only a firm will
can keep him steadfast under fire.   It would
be futile to wonder how a Parisian novelist
would have treated the relations of Jack and
Carmen, but it may be doubted whether that
treatment would be as calmly truthful as
Mr. Warner's.   The American author knew his
type when he made Henderson conscious that
Carmen was as "passionless as a diamond."

How true to life Carmen may be, and how
accurate Edith Delancy, I do not know ; for
how is a mere man to decide on the niceties
of feminine character ?   Every novel really
worth criticising needs two critics—a man to
discuss the male characters, and a woman to

discuss the female. It is easy enough for any
man to say that the heroes of many women's
novels are impossible, for the most part either
prigs or brutes; but may not the women
retort on us, and declare the irresistible
heroines of men's novels equally impossible?
To us men Carmen is coherent and convincing; Edith Delancy is almost flawless, and
quite too good for that very human creature
Jack; Dr. Ruth Leigh is most sympatheti-
cally drawn; but what do the women think of
these creatures of a masculine brain? I can
bear testimony to the dignity and the strength
with which father Damon is delineated; but
I lack the knowledge to take the stand in
behalf of Dr. Ruth, who seems to me quite as
well conceived, and quite as happily presented.

In this his third work of fiction the author
is more the master of the art than in the
earlier studies. He possesses his materials
now; he is not possessed by them. He keeps
his story more firmly in hand; the construction is solider; the movement is swifter; and
there are fewer digressions from the main path.
To a certain extent the modern novel is the
result of a marriage of the essay and the
drama; and it is natural enough that the
child should resemble now one of the parents
and now the other. In Mr. Warner's hands, as
was to be expected, the tendency is rather

S

toward the essay, yet there is no obtrusion of
the narrator's personality, and there is no lack
of dramatic force in certain of the situations.
In more than one of them—in the parting of
the doctor and the priest, for example—there
is the swift simplicity of tragedy, inevitable,
inexorable, final.